Not the Time to Stay:
The Unpublished Plays
of Víctor Fragoso

Not the Time to Stay: The Unpublished Plays of Víctor Fragoso

Víctor Fragoso
Edited, translated and with an Introduction
by Consuelo Martínez-Reyes

Library of Congress Cataloging-in-Publication Data

Names: Fragoso, Víctor, 1944-1982, author. | Martínez-Reyes, Consuelo,
    editor, translator, writer of introduction.
Title: Not the time to stay : the unpublished plays of Víctor Fragoso /
    selected, edited, translated and with an introduction by Consuelo
    Martínez-Reyes.
Description: New York, NY : Centro Press, Center for Puerto Rican Studies,
    Hunter College, CUNY, [2018] | Includes bibliographical references and
    index.
Identifiers: LCCN 2018034538 (print) | LCCN 2018045062 (ebook) | ISBN
    9781945662256 | ISBN 9781945662249 | ISBN 9781945662249 (paperback
    : alk. paper) | ISBN 9781945662256 (ebook)
Subjects: | LCGFT: Drama.
Classification: LCC PQ7440.F68 (ebook) | LCC PQ7440.F68 A6 2018 (print) | DDC
    862/.64--dc23
LC record available at https://lccn.loc.gov/2018034538

Published by
Centro Press
Center for Puerto Rican Studies
Hunter College, CUNY
695 Park Avenue, E-1429
New York, NY 10065
centrops@hunter.cuny.edu
http://centropr.hunter.cuny.edu

Printed in the United States of America on acid-free paper.

From the Víctor Fragoso Collection. The Center for Puerto Rican Studies Library and Archives. Hunter College, CUNY.

TABLE OF CONTENTS

ACKNOWLEDGEMENTS

This project would not have been possible without the willingness of the Fragoso family to share the work of their loved one with the rest of us. I would like to thank them first and foremost. My greatest appreciation to Carmen Delia Fernández Fragoso, Millie Reyes, and Delia María Cruz Fernández. Thank you for honoring me with your trust. I hope I have made justice to Víctor Fragoso's oeuvre. Secondly but not far behind, I would like to thank the Director of the Center for Puerto Rican Studies, Edwin Meléndez, who believed in this project from the get go and gave wings to my relentless wish to have the new generation of Latinos get to know Fragoso's work.

I would like to say thank you to all the Centro team for their feedback and support: Xavier Totti, Noraliz Ruiz, Harry Franqui-Rivera, Marilisa Jimenez-Garcia, Carlos Vargas-Ramos, José de Jesús, Pedro Juan Hernández, Alberto Hernández. You are undoubtedly the best academic family one could ask for, and I will always consider myself the luckiest to have had my career start as a postdoctoral fellow at Centro.

Speaking of family, my infinite gratitude goes to my partner in life, Ben Mercer, for the many nights he heard me talk endlessly about this project, and for supporting me unconditionally and in so many ways; and to my daughter, Isabela, for patiently 'sharing' me with Fragoso.

Lastly, I would like to dedicate this book to the many Puerto Ricans and Latinos who live in New York City, as well as in the rest of the United States. I am certain Fragoso wrote these plays thinking of you, of what affects you and worries you, about what makes you laugh and think. And it is thus my honor to get these back to you.

INTRODUCTION:
THE LIFE AND THEATER OF VÍCTOR FRAGOSO
By Consuelo Martínez-Reyes

October 15, 1980
El Barrio

Dear Mother,

These days, I've been stuck to the typewriter...
It may sound crazy, but sometimes one must
take drastic decisions if one wants to work on
something that truly satisfies you.

—Víctor Fragoso

I open with a fragment of one of Víctor Fernández Fragoso's letter to his mother, Concepción (Concha) Fragoso. I discovered these letters going through the voluminous collection the Fragoso family recently donated to the Center for Puerto Rican Studies' Archives of the Diaspora. Víctor Fragoso's letters to his mother are oftentimes similar to the reflection diaries he kept. He shared with her his plans and dreams, the moments he valued. In this letter, he speaks about his decision to dedicate his sabbatical from his position as Assistant Professor of Spanish at Livingston College, a Rutgers University campus, entirely to creative writing. Like many creative academics, Fragoso must have been torn between utilising his time to produce analytical work that moves us up the ladder in the academic world, or, as he decidedly opted to, to spend it giving in to the forces of imagination, despite the fact that creative work often goes unrecognized in the field. His work as poet and playwright was a way to share his talent with everyday Puerto Ricans, and not just with those attending Livingston College, but above all, it was the passion that moved him.

Víctor Fragoso was born on January 14, 1944 in Río Piedras, Puerto Rico. In 1965, after completing a Bachelor's degree in Biology at the University of Puerto Rico, Fragoso moved to New York City, following a job as a research assistant at the Memorial Sloan Kettering Cancer Center. But before leaving the island, Fragoso had already made his mark as a poet. He won a poetry award by presenting his still unpublished poetry collection *MAR* [SEA] to the Ateneo Puertorriqueño. Similarly, in 1967 he won the poetry award at the Círculo de Escritores y Poetas Iberoamericanos.

It becomes unsurprising then that in that same year he left the position at Sloan Ketting to dedicate his life to literature, commencing a PhD at the University of Connecticut, Storrs. There, his doctoral dissertation focused on Dominican Pedro Mir, a poet from the Hispanic Caribbean region, like himself.

Fragoso spent sixteen years moving between Connecticut, New Jersey, and New York, making sure to keep an active engagement with his community in the East Coast region of the United States. He became Assistant Professor of Spanish at Livingston College in 1970, while also keeping an active profile as a poet and playwright. He published two poetry collections while he was still with us: in 1973, *El reino de la espiga: Canto al coraje de Walt y Federico* (Colección Nuevasangre, New York), followed by *Ser islas/Being Islands* in 1976 (Editorial Libro Viaje, New York). And while his poetry was highly commended when it was first published, with Fragoso's passing, it has been understudied throughout the years, only with a few scholars such as Efraín Barradas, Carlos Rodríguez Matos, Chiqui Vicioso, María Canino and Rubén Ríos Ávila to remind us of his excelling work. More recently, Ángel Antonio Ruiz edited Fragoso's two previous poetry books in the collection *Poesía completa*, under Editorial Erizo. It follows that, at least to those who did not live with him in New York, Fragoso was mainly known as a poet. But those in the city witnessed his laborious and relentless undertakings with the Puerto Rican theater community.

Fragoso's plays were presented at DUO Theater (New York) and the Riviera Theater (Puerto Rico), among other spaces. He wrote and directed for theatre groups such as Teatro Orilla (1970-1972) and Teatro 4 (1980), and was involved in different ways with Teatro Pregones, Teatro Pobre de América, INTAR, and the Puerto Rican Traveling Theater. In 1972, he founded Grupo Guazábara, through which students put together plays based on the realities lived by Puerto Ricans in the East Coast and presented them at public spaces such as schools and community centers. He also founded the Puerto Rican Theater Collective in 1979, and co-founded Nuevasangre [New Blood] a poetry group centered on Hispanic American poets, serving as co-editor of its homonymous magazine. After reviewing the overwhelming list of tasks he kept within the theater community, one can see theater was his true passion.

Thus, when presented with the opportunity to make some of the unpublished material available to the public, as editor and translator, I decided to begin with what has remained 'unknown,' his theater. This anthology includes eight of Fragoso's unpublished plays, presented in the following order: *Not the Time to Stay* (undated), *Call my Number* (1977), *Santaclos in Borinkén* (1979), *Undecided, from Cayey* (1979), *Don't Get Nervous* (undated), *Newark, 1974* (1974), *The Latino Era* (co-written with Dolores Prida) (1980), and *First Night Out: The Basic Training of a Bag Lady* (1981). As it can be noted, the works are not presented in chronological order but rather follow a thematic flow that moves from the personal to the universal, and that simultaneously splits the book in the two places that constituted Fragoso's home: the first four plays mainly take place in Puerto Rico, while the last four are located in New York City.

This project is evidence of Fragoso's ceaseless dedication to both theater and his people. Like Vanessa Droz and Rubén Ríos Ávila have already pointed out, Fragoso shared with his generation a preoccupation for national and societal issues, and his plays are no exception to this. In his "Notas sobre la expresión teatral de la comunidad puertorriqueña" [Notes on the Theater Activity of the Puerto Rican Community], Fragoso marks the sixties as the decade in which the Latino community develops a constant presence in the New York City theater scene. Fragoso signals René Marqués' *La carreta* as a key play for the diasporic community. First presented in 1953, not in Puerto Rico, but in New York's Hunts Points Palace, the play stages the story of a family displaced from the island's countryside to the metropolitan area, and their eventual move to New York City, all in search of better life conditions. In many ways, Fragoso's work must be seen in conversation with that of Marqués. Both portray the real lives and harsh realities of Puerto Ricans living in the USA.

It is interesting that Marqués' work reappears in the city in 1965, when it is presented at the Greenwich Mews Theater for an English-speaking audience. In 1966, funded by various state agencies, The Puerto Rican Traveling Theater also performs *La carreta* in different Puerto Rican neighborhoods. This reminds us of the 'travels' of some of Fragoso's plays, specifically those of *The Latino Era*, which was presented throughout New York City in Spanish, English, or Spanglish, depending on the linguistic attributes Fragoso found belonged to each neighbourhood. Eva C. Vásquez looks at the history of the Pregones Theater in order to portray how "Puerto Rican theater, which emphasizes its own power to represent the people's desire for social change, may be a tool in developing a positive image of Puerto Rican culture and people" (2003, 6). Fragoso certainly had similar goals in mind: to demand social transformation and reaffirm our love for Puerto Rican culture. In both his chosen themes and linguistic practices, Fragoso stays true to his goal of pushing forth and portraying change within his community.

But he did this in extremely creative and varied ways. While some of his plays keep in obvious conversation with canonical Puerto Rican literature, others look toward the future, questioning the limits of genres and blurring the line between the real and fiction. In this sense, his plays are much in line with the way in which Vásquez summarizes Puerto Rican theater: "Since the sixties, Puerto Rican theater has reflected the impact of the world's political events, emphasizing a tendency toward social realism, psychological awareness and, more recently, the absurd" (2003, 11). Many of the plays included in the anthology portray these tendencies, in addition to showing a commonality of themes in issues of gender, homosexuality, and life in the diaspora, as I have discussed elsewhere.

After interviewing some of Fragoso's relatives and friends, I believe these aspects of everyday life were close to his heart. The insistence with which gender imbalance and injustice toward woman appears in his oeuvre is testimony of his love for his mother, Doña Conchita. According to Carmen Delia Fernández, Víctor Fernández Fragoso's sister, the poet opted to go by his mother's last name, Fragoso, instead of the paternal surname, as is customary, because of his close relationship to his mother, and his admiration for her active role in his upbringing. Mili Fernández, Carmen Delia's daughter and Víctor Fragoso's niece and godchild, considers there was almost a symbolic homage to the love between Fragoso and his mother in the way in which Doña Conchita passed away shortly after her son. Both Mili and Carmen Delia recall Fragoso's illness as an uncertain process, and the hopes of him getting through it. Two days shy of turning 38, Víctor Fragoso passed away on January 12, 1982, one of the early victims of what we would come to know as AIDS. Carmen Delia remembers how Fragoso's death was devastating for his family, in line with the shattering experience of a whole generation that saw the appearance of the deadly AIDS virus. His body was brought to the island, but there was only a shy mention of his passing in the island's press, while the community in New York City prepared various homages in his name.

Mili got to know New York City and all the artistic activity of the place with her uncle in her summer visits. She remembers a family that celebrated Fragoso whenever he came back to the island, had no issues with his sexuality (although it was not talked about much), and an uncle who openly spent time with his partner in New York. Carmen Delia confirmed that Fragoso left the island because to be gay in Puerto Rico was taboo, and mentioned that despite being surrounded by what came to be our great talents in the diaspora, such as Clemente Soto Vélez and Manuel Ramos Otero, the poet and playwright was very humble about it all, and felt in his element in the city.

Efraín Barradas and María Canino describe Fragoso as a very private man and this is reflected in his literature. When it comes to the portrayal of gay issues in his work, Barradas says, "it is there, but it is a private world." Both Barradas and Canino have told me of Fragoso's handsomeness and charming personality, but also about his striking humility. His family and friends all see reflected in his work his experiences of the intimate, of isolation at a personal and national level, of migration, his sexuality, and the political movements that marked his youth. As I talked to all of them, I realized how Fragoso managed to let us all into his world when we read him.

I here try to further open than window into his world as I briefly discuss each play as a means of introduction to their attributes, in hopes of guiding the reader through Fragoso's oeuvre. This is not an exhaustive study of his work but rather a sketch to promote future analysis of his plays. Similarly, as a translation scholar, I understand the benefit of providing commentary regarding the decisions made to bring his work into English. While space limitations forbid a thorough discussion of these, I try to mention key points that came up in translating Víctor Fragoso's theater. Still a graduate student, I began doing translation work pro-bono for different small organizations. This steered me to opportunities such as working with PBS and the National Council of La Raza, among others. Most specially, it led me to this project. By the time the Fragoso manuscripts were on my hands, I felt confidently able to bring them all back to us in English. Yet, as any translator, I can only hope I achieved something resembling the original. The goal of sharing an oeuvre that would otherwise remain hidden to the wider public pushed me in times of struggle.

One of Fragoso's plays was written entirely in English, while some were heavily influenced by it or written in both English and Spanish. There my work was mainly that of an editor. Most of his plays were written in Spanish, which offered the liberty to think of the piece as a whole and offer something similar. Yet all of them portray the bilingual context in which they were born, have bilingual jokes and assume a bicultural (Latino/American) background. Instances in which such bilingual context became obvious were the hardest to translate and yet left me most in awe of Fragoso's talent. His ability to play with language is something I aimed to replicate. Norma Helsper (1992) has already noted that we need to go beyond 'translating words' in order to convey what is, in the case of Fragoso's plays, a bicultural and bilingual culture.

I see my work here as an intermediary tool between the playwright who is no longer with us, and the contemporary Latino, the director, or teacher who would like to get closer to our past theatre movements and ideas, which I have tried to incorporate in my translation choices. Lawrence Venuti has correctly noted that,

translating is always ideological because it releases a domestic remainder, an inscription of values, beliefs, and representations linked to historical moments and social positions in the receiving culture. In serving domestic interests, a translation provides an ideological resolution for the linguistic and cultural differences of the foreign text. (2004, 498)

In translating Víctor Fragoso's plays, I certainly confronted ideological issues. Not only is his work already political, sometimes more openly than others, but also language itself functions as a political tool in many instances. Changing from Spanish to English, from English to Spanish, or mixing the two, his characters remind us they are migrants whose mother tongue is considered an outsider. Language is also reflective of the generational differences between characters. Fragoso tried to portray the fact that those who had been born and raised in New York City would mainly express themselves in English, while living in a Spanish-speaking context which included their parents, whose native language was Spanish, as well as those who had recently moved to the city from Puerto Rico and/or other Spanish-speaking countries. Similarly, I tried to keep to the speech rhythm Fragoso posed upon his characters, which can sometimes be fast, and at others, staccatoed. Lastly, as I am aware that directors make their plays their own, this text has been produced with the reader in mind. Thus, while I may have considered 'speakability' to an extent, this aspect was not the main focus in the translation, but rather to stay true to Fragoso's style and ideas.

The collection opens with a piece where varied key trends in Latino theater coincide. *Not the Time to Stay* markedly reflects on the implications of the psychological upon our memories and future plans, and has moments palpably inspired by the theater of the absurd. The play represents two couples performed by the same two actors, a certain challenge to be staged with only the most talented artists. The relationships between Moncho and his wife Hilda, together with that of their son Jaime and his wife, blur together. This aspect of the play promises an investigation from an oedipal perspective as it becomes clear the roles of wife and mother, and husband and son, are socially exchangeable in many ways. This is probably due to the fixed gender expectations that persist throughout generations, as evidenced by the very contemporary feel in Fragoso's play.

The play presents the erosion of these relationships and the male characters' considerations to leave for New York City, shrouding the place with a cloud of uncertainty that reflects upon the meaning of the diasporic experience for both those who leave and those who stay, a topic that proves relevant as Puerto Rico currently undergoes a massive migratory wave due to the effects of Hurricane Maria on the island. A fifth 'character,' Jaime's mirror image, will surely serve some Lacanian considerations, as well as reflections on the public and the private, and the links between physical sameness and homosexuality previously established by scholars such as Juan Duchesne Winter.

The passing of time and timing, as its title indicates, is also pivotal to the analysis of the play. The piece opens with a Hilda that is threatening to leave because "It's 3:10, not the time to stay," and Jaime's obsession with time obliges Hilda to later state it is (only) 3:25, despite the fact that the play navigates the evolution of two generations of love affairs traversed by power dynamics ruled by gender expectations, and migration. Lastly, Puerto Rican independence from the United States is also a subject within Fragoso's work and it surely affects the interactions between Moncho and his son. *Not the Time to Stay* is perhaps Fragoso's invitation for action, a request for mobilization, literal—through migration, and metaphorical—through our probing of hegemonic discourse on nationalism and gender.

I decided to open the anthology with this play not only because, despite its brevity, it gathers theatrical characteristics that the reader, as they journey through the compilation, will find to be recognizably Fragoso's, but also because it embodies his world vision and his preoccupation with pushing his audience to question the limitations of our societal expectations and demands, and ultimately, of ourselves.

Much has been written about celebrated Puerto Rican poet, Julia de Burgos, and it often used to encircle her life in a myth of martyrdom. It took thirteen years after de Burgos' passing for Yvette Jiménez de Báez to come up with a biography that questioned the marred version of the poet's experience of love, as well as life in the United States.[1] Fragoso seems to follow Jiménez' steps in his play *Call my Number*, a piece inspired on Julia de Burgos' life in which he collates her poems and letters to her sister Consuelo to construct a version of her life through her own words.[2] *Call my Number* is a two-actress play in which a healthy Julia declaims poetry while a weak, silent, and dancing Julia mirrors the narrative. The piece defies death to 'call her number,' and portrays the poet's adversities while emphasizing her resilience.

Fragoso's work uses de Burgos' poems to present her childhood and her transition into adulthood, and compliments this with her letters as a means to express the poet's thoughts on love, politics, and migration. We must acknowledge the connection between such collocation of poems and letters and the Theater of the Real (Ibsen, Chekov), as well as other traits within the play, like its focus on symbolism and minimalistic staging. There is certain potential here for scholars to investigate these links, among other aspects of the piece. Such is the case with the explicit and implicit ways in which *Call my Number* and its related paraphernalia touch on the subject of independence for the island. The hand program for the play, written by Maria Coles, traces similarities between Julia de Burgos and Welsh poet Dylan Thomas, implicating political issues (between Wales and the United Kingdom, Puerto Rico and the United States) are to blame for the 'doomed' life of these poets. The program for the play is one example of the various archival materials now available at the Center for Puerto Rican Studies archives and that remain to be explored in order to trace larger socio-political connections that now inform decolonial and postcolonial thought.

Named after one of de Burgos' own poems, the play was staged in 1977 in a small Lower East Side theater by the Duo/Spanish-English Ensemble. Duo Theater was located in Manhattan's Lower East Side, and as its name indicates, was one of the few of its kind to stage plays in both Spanish and English. It thus functioned as a meeting place for the various Hispanic communities in the city and likely aided in the promotion of Julia de Burgos as an icon for PanLatinidad. Iris Zavala-Martínez, Vanessa Pérez Rosario, and Oscar Montero have sketched out the ways in which de Burgos' work signals future difficulties for PanLatinos in New York City. Víctor Fragoso portrays our Julia as part of that bridge that connects the past and present of the diasporic communities and their fight for civil rights in the U.SA. and reconfigures the narrative around her diasporic experience. Although Fragoso's approach reinvents New York City as a positive environment, he does not erase the troubles the poet encountered. The playwright presents de Burgos in light of her mental illness and, if anything, as a victim of depression, not love. The city is not to blame for her demise, but rather where it takes place.

While some of Fragoso's plays, such as *Not the Time to Stay, Undecided, from Cayey*, and *Don't Get Nervous* were written entirely in Spanish, *Call My Number* is one of those which mixed languages, in this instance by keeping Julia de Burgos' poems in their original (mostly Spanish, except her last poem) but having stage directions in English. Here, I decided not to consult existing translations of de Burgos' poems as to avoid being influenced by them, and aimed to present the poems through Fragoso's aesthetics and way of thinking. I see the goal in this case is not necessarily to transmit de Burgos' style and words but the way in which Fragoso saw them.

Similarly, *Santaclos in Borinken* uses both English and Spanish. The play is mostly in English but brings comedic aspects through language misunderstandings between monolinguals. Despite the fact that Víctor Fragoso subtitled this work as a 'cartoon' (*un dibujo animado*), the piece follows the traditional structure and characteristics of a play. We can't find, among the materials in the archive, proof that this play ever made it to stage, print or TV. It will be in the hand of scholars to interview Fragoso's contemporaries and seek further to find out. What is clear from *Santaclos in Borinken* is that the playwright produced a piece of work in line with the traditional Puerto Rican Christmas play, in which the audience becomes another actor. Here, the magic of the holidays remains untouched for the little ones, while a subtext of comedic political and social criticism entertains the adults. One can certainly envision this play becoming a classic in schools and holiday community functions, especially those that close with the traditional gift giving by the Three Wise Men.

Fragoso's Christmas piece reminds us of the canonical *Santacló va a la cuchilla* [Santacló visits Cuchilla] by Puerto Rican writer Abelardo Díaz Alfaro, in which tradition and the force of rapid modernization that came with Operation Bootstrap become intertwined to warn us about an impending cultural shift and portray the never-ending sociocultural tensions between Puerto Rico and the United States. *Santaclos in Borinken* also winks at those historical days in which San Juan's legendary mayor, Felisa Rincón de Gautier, better known as Doña Fela, adorned our tropical islander Christmas with snow.

Santaclos in Borinken portrays Santa Claus' supposed first visit to Puerto Rico. Worried that the children of the island have already heard of his existence, Santa looks to 'expand' his world coverage by paying them a visit that goes wrong in all sorts of ways, from bad weather, to encounters with the police, and of course, language difficulties. These mishaps function as a way to make evident the lack of cultural awareness and overall knowledge of Puerto Rico by Santa Claus, who symbolically stands in for Americans. In contrast, the Three Wise Men, who already visit the island on a regular basis, come to the rescue when things turn awry for Santa. Santa cannot speak the language, nor find our chimneys, and is evidently unprepared for the tropical weather. The play brings to the fore various political aspects relevant to the island's colonial situation and issues of acculturation.

In addition, Santaclos' approach to Christmas is marred by the cons of modernity: overproduction, overworked employees, and an obsession to grow his 'business' and reputation. He speaks of "expansion" and refers to his abode as his "factory." English fluency is also presented as a class marker, as a Puerto Rican wealthy kid writing in English confesses that in his private Catholic school he is taught that "it is very important to learn English if you want to get a good job." But on a more positive note, Fragoso's play touches on the mainland versus island 'divide' by including our diasporic communities in Santa's new route, thus expanding the limits of *puertorriqueñidad* and/or *latinidad* to one that is not based on language nor location but rather on culture.

Some words in *Santaclos in Borinken* were left in Spanish for reasons pertaining to culture and their double meaning. *Santaclos, borinken, parranda* and *asalto* are good examples. *Santaclos* is a transliteration of the Puerto Rican pronunciation of Santa Claus, but most importantly, it is reminiscent of the canonical short story *Santacló va a La Cuchilla*, which Fragoso's play evidently intends as background context. *Borinken*, the taíno name for Puerto Rico, functions in a similar way in that it brings the island's native history back into the present. *Parranda* was left in Spanish as it carries a different cultural meaning than that of 'Christmas carols', which would be the closest to an English equivalent. *Parrandas* are livelier in spirit and require the element of surprise, which is key for the comedic events that take place in the play. It follows that this is why *asalto*, which can be translated both as 'assault' and something akin to 'surprise', was also kept in Spanish. 'Asalto' is what Puerto Ricans offering a *parranda* yell upon their arrival to a house, to startle its inhabitants before they start singing. But its literal translation by Rudolph and his lack of cultural understanding, brings light upon the lack of knowledge of Puerto Rican culture by the (symbolically American) reindeer. As a translator myself, I loved this scene with Rudolph since it serves as a great example of how translation cannot be done without a considerable familiarity with both the source and target cultures.

A common question among students of translation that quickly comes to mind is how much creative liberty can we have as translators. I have always recommended to use creativity wisely: it is a tool that, as such, can both help us build as well as destroy. We must behave as painting curators in our aim to recreate what we know is underneath. There were a couple of instances in which creativity was required of me, but I stayed close to my knowledge of Fragoso's work in these occasions. For example, the descriptions of the three wise men in *Santaclos in Borinken* were written by me, following Fragoso's notes on the original manuscript: "they each give a brief biographical speech." Similarly, there was only a description provided for the content of "The island of enchantment" song. I felt the need to provide a song and thus created one in keeping with Fragoso's usual emphasis on rhythm and rhyme.

Lastly, the play closes with the Puerto Rican *aguinaldo* (Christmas song), "De tierra lejana." I did consult an existing translation of this song by George K. Evans and Walter Ehret,[3] which was produced to be sung by a church choir in 1963. I did this thinking that I should opt for an existing translation if available since it may circulate as a canonical English version. Finding that the few existing versions were in fact very varied amongst themselves, and that they all satisfied the needs of Christmas celebrations within the church, I embarked in the adventure of creating my own translation. It is my opinion that Fragoso would have opted for the song to be sung in its original Spanish, but if language practices made that difficult, he would have preferred a version such as the one I provided: one that emphasises on what has been termed the 'pentathlon principle' of song translation by Peter Low (2005). Low looks at 'singability' (where words are easy to sing to particular notes), rhyme, rhythm, naturalness, and fidelity to the ideas presented in the source text. All these aspects, I am confident, where important to Fragoso as a playwright and director, as well as to me as a translator. Lexical accessibility was also key here, provided children are the intended target audience.

At the other end of the spectrum, *Undecided, from Cayey* takes us to the harsh realities of everyday life. In the hopes of receiving confirmation that she should leave her abusive husband, Clara writes to the host of the *Just for you, ladies* radio show. But, signalling the perpetuation of traditional mores that endanger victims of domestic violence, the presenter encourages to find solace in the bible, and to check her 'tone of voice' when she talks to her husband. To make matters worse, Clara receives the visit of Miguelito, a supposed friend of her husband who lets himself into the house only to abuse her. Their interaction, and her husband's reactions to the events reveal much about the contradictory position in which many women find themselves when following social expectations of obedience and housekeeping. The play opens up many issues, from the role of religion in gender inequalities to how social hypocrisy enables the oppression of women.

In a similar thematic trend, *Don't Get Nervous* consists of two independent interludes joint under the same title and therefore overall subject: oppression directed towards gays, in the first instance, and women in the second. In the first interlude, Vicente hears his best friend confess his love for him. Vicente's reaction opens the doors to questions about homosexual identity (vis a vis practices) and 'passing.' The second interlude presents Moncho, a stereotypical macho who kills his girlfriend upon learning she was not a virgin when they met. Moncho's travels down memory lane allows us to recognize the warning signs of his hostile behaviour and exposes issues of gender expectations and inequalities that indirectly support violence against women.

The lack of a voice for minorities as an issue becomes larger within the anthology as Fragoso recovers a chapter in our history that threatens to be forgotten. Natalie Delgadillo has recently pointed out the erasure of historical uprisings by the Puerto Rican population in the United States. The events that took place in the Puerto Rican Festival celebrated at Branch Brook Park in Newark on September 1st, 1974 are part of such obliteration. In his interview for the New Jersey Latino Oral History Project, community member William Q. Sánchez points out that "there are people still today who say there were no riots in 1974. Obviously, no one wants to—can explain the trampling of people by policeman and horses, the people who died in the streets" (Matta 2012, 2). Sánchez refers to the events that Víctor Fragoso tried to reconstruct in *Newark, 1974.*

Commonly referred to as "The 1974 riots," the phrase commemorates the day when the *fiestas patronales* celebrated by the Puerto Rican community in Branch Brook Park were ruined by a confrontation between the attendees and the policemen in horses patrolling the event. Leaders of the Latino community reacted to this by talking to then mayor Kenneth A. Gibson, but not much was achieved and the *fiestas* were suspended from that moment on. To counter the obliteration of Latino history, past Rutgers University history professor Dr. Olga Jiménez de Wagenheim recently founded the New Jersey Hispanic Research Information Center (Carter 2016). More pertinent to us, Jiménez de Wagenheim also organized the traveling exhibit "Newark '74: Remembering the Puerto Rican Riots—An Unexamined History." Since then, Yesenia López and Elizabeth Parker have brought it to Bloomfield College and The Newark Public Library. Fragoso now joins the social and artistic initiatives, such as the New Jersey Hispanic Research Information Center, the New Jersey Latino Oral

History Project, and the *Newark '74 Riots* traveling exhibit in the remembrance of the positive and negative results of moments like these within Latino history.

Another relevant aspect of Latino history that features in the anthology is that of the unification of the separate countries that constitute the Hispanic world into "one" Latino community in the United States. The problematic American obsession to narrow down the Latino identity to just one is both criticised and exploited for marketing (and comedic) purposes within the play *The Latino Era*, co-written with Cuban-American Dolores Prida. But a sympathetic recognition of points of encounter amongst Latin American cultures also serves as a reason for an alliance between the characters, one that mirrors some of the initiatives that took place during the 1960s civil rights movements and that still holds in place today.

Fragoso and Prida's *The Latino Era* is a comedic and multifaceted play that aims to discuss the complexity of the Latino identity. The plot revolves around Chago's effort to write a Broadway musical that would capture the essence of being Latino in the United States, all in one night. A schizophrenic and hilarious experience ensues. The stage is divided in two, where half of it portrays Chago and his friend coming up with ideas to write, while the other half presents actors trying to bring them to life by enacting them. The play cleverly moves between the negative stereotypes surrounding the Latino population and the positivity of moving toward achieving the 'American dream.' In *Coser y cantar*, Dolores Prida uses similar linguistic and staging techniques. A split stage and code-switching enables the mirroring of the Spanish and English languages and their corresponding personalities within the mind of She/Ella. Each of her halves represents an ethnic stereotyped related to the language it speaks. I am certain that a comparative study between the theatrical styles of Víctor Fragoso and Dolores Prida, as well as how these come together in *The Latino Era*, will be required homework for scholars.

Language in the text becomes a playground in which Fragoso toys with the linguistic practices of the communities in which the play was staged. The Center for Puerto Rican Studies Archives currently holds three discernible versions of *La era latina*. At first, the pattern is unclear, but the dutiful eye can take note of various consistencies amongst them: (1) stage directions always appear in English, (2) younger characters communicate mostly in English, while (3) older characters either use Spanish or vacillate between Spanish and English. To satisfy monolinguals of Spanish and English, Fragoso's characters repeat phrases in both languages. This 'instant translation' within the play is obviously lost in the English-only version presented here. But other aspects of the play's translation show to be significantly more difficult to handle. Namely, Fragoso's use of bilingual puns and common sayings, as well as references to cultural practices and food mostly identifiable within a Latino context but that may be unknown to other cultures. One amongst these is Fragoso's use of "tostones" within the play. *Tostones* are a well-known dish within the Hispanic culture, consisting of flattened, yet thick, fried plantains. Also known as *patacones* in Colombia, or *fritos verdes* in the Dominican Republic, among other names, *tostones* serve as a metaphor for Latinos within the play, demonstrating that although the substance may seem similar, (identity and culture) content is perceived and handled differently within each country, and must sadly be renamed and marketed as one unique product in order for it to be successful in the United States. Due to the long discussion around their meaning, and the implicit explanation of the food item, I kept the original Spanish *tostones* in the play, since it evidently enriches the multiple interpretations of the piece.

First Night Out: The Basic Training of a Bag Lady is the only play written originally and completely in English. Subtitled, "A comedy with musical implications," the piece is comedic in tone and includes various songs. In this instance, the plot moves beyond issues that mostly affect the Latino community to focus on homelessness, a problem that concerns the city of New York as a whole. Street-dwellers Leonor, Angela, and Virginia, talk to Madeline, who tries to pass as a journalist during her first night living in the streets.

First Night Out was mainly an editing task as it was originally written in English in its entirety. Dated 1981, we can suspect it was one of Fragoso's last works. But not with complete certainty, as some of Fragoso's plays were not dated and he passed away in 1982. The fact that it was written completely in English adds to my suspicion that this was, in fact, one of his latest work, and it makes me wonder if he would have eventually crossed over into the wider, English-speaking market. As I sifted through the playwright's notes and sketches, I understood the basis for his language evolution. Among the plays we received from the Fragoso family, the earliest were written in Spanish, while the latest navigated both Spanish and English. In cases where multiple versions of the same play were available, like that of *La era latina* (*The Latino Era*), earlier versions are mainly written in Spanish, while the later ones were heavily influenced by English, or shall we say, written in Spanglish.

As we see Fragoso shifting from the Spanish to the English language, we could argue that something similar takes place with the topics concerning his plays, moving from the local to the global. If this move is rightly perceived and intentionally so, then *La era latina* and *First Night Out* would be placed at the end of the spectrum. Both texts focus on the societal repercussions of prejudice against minorities such as Latinos and the homeless. *First Night Out* reassures us that Fragoso had become comfortable with writing in English, and that he was overall concerned about issues that affected not only his people but also humanity at large.

As Translation Studies move forward, practitioners become more aware of the benefits of case studies, of sharing our thought processes, our difficulties, and limitations, be those linguistic or cultural in nature. I write these pages in an effort to shed light to the challenges of dealing with both bilingual texts and drama, fields in which there is still much terrain unexplored. My presentation of translation issues here has not been systematic in any way, but rather a reflection and exploration into these texts and the questions they pose, in the hope that translators in similar situations have the opportunity to deliberate on how to move the field forward.

The same could be said about the place of this anthology within fields such as Puerto Rican and Latino Studies. While my presentation of Fragoso's life and theater is fairly comprehensive, the main purpose here is to set a basis from which to explore his works further. Students and scholars interested in Víctor Fragoso's oeuvre should visit the Center for Puerto Rican Studies archives and consult the variety of raw materials available for an unforgettable experience. Similarly, I am sure that theater lovers will enjoy this collection and look forward to seeing these plays on stage.

NOTES

1 More contemporary scholarship by María Solá, Juan Gelpí, Rubén Ríos Ávila, and Vanessa Pérez Rosario further support such break with patriarchal tendencies that victimized the poet.

2 It is important to note that Fragoso only had access to the letters included in de Báez' work. Fragoso was related to Julia de Burgos, as his mother was de Burgos' first cousin. But the two never met nor can we confirm access to the original letters by Fragoso (in interview with Millie Reyes, family member). De Burgos was in New York while Fragoso was in Puerto Rico, and she passed away in 1953, before he moved to the city in 1965.

3 "De tierra lejana venimos a verte" (From a distant land home of the Savior we come seeking). Trans. By Geoge K. Evans and Walter Ehret. <https://hymnary.org/text/from_a_distant_home_the_savior_we_come/>.

REFERENCES

Carter, Barry. 2016. Newark archivist revives lost history of Puerto Rican riots. *NJ.com* 1 March. <http://www.nj.com/essex/index.ssf/2016/03/newark_archivist_revives_lost_history_of_puerto_ri.html/>.

Delgadillo, Natalie. 2017 The Forgotten History of Latino Riots. *CityLab* (from *The Atlantic*) 11 April. <https://www.citylab.com/politics/2017/04/the-forgotten-history-of-latino-riots/522570/>.

Droz, Vanessa. 1982. Testimonio de la labor literaria de Víctor Fragoso. *El Mundo* 11 February.

Duchesne Winter, Juan. 1996. "Prótesis" y "Acariciarás al objeto como a ti mismo (Para un cuerpo inhumano)." In *Política de la caricia: ensayos sobre la corporalidad, erotismo, literatura y poder*. 1–47. Río Piedras: Libros Nómadas y Decanato de Estudios Graduados e Investigación de la Universidad de Puerto Rico.

Fragoso. Víctor. 1976. Notas sobre la expression teatral de la comunidad puertorriqueña de Nueva York. *Revista del Instituto de Cultura Puertorriqueña* 70(enero-marzo), 21–6.

Helpser, Norma. 1992. Biculturalism for Survival: Two Plays by Dolores Prida. Paper read at Latin American Theatre Today: History, Gender, Genre and Performance. University of Kansas, 30 April.

Low, Peter. 2005. The Pentathlon Approach to Translating Songs. In *Song and Significance: Virtues and Vices of Vocal Translation*, ed. Dinda L. Gorlée. 185–212. Amsterdam: Rodopi.

Martínez-Reyes, Consuelo. 2017. Gender, Homosexuality, the Diasporic Experience, and Other Key Themes in Víctor Fragoso's Theater. *CENTRO: Journal of the Center for Puerto Rican Studies* 29(2), 106–35.

Matta, Karlha. 2012. William Sanchez Interview, Part II. New Jersey Latino Oral History Project. Available at The Newark Public Library. <https://www.npl.org/Pages/Collections/njhric/Sanchez2_iti.pdf/>.

Prida, Dolores. 1991. *Beautiful Señoritas and Other Plays*. Houston: Arte Público Press.

Ríos Ávila, Rubén. 2012. El ser isla de Víctor Fragoso. *80grados* 20 April. <http://www.80grados.net/el-ser-isla-de-victor-fragoso/>.

Vásquez, Eva C. 2003. *Pregones Theater: A theater for Social Change in the South Bronx*. New York: Routledge.

Venuti, Lawrence. 2004. Translation, Community, Utopia. In *The Translation Studies Reader*. 2nd edition., ed. Lawrence Venuti. 482–501. New York: Routledge.

PLAYS

From the Víctor Fragoso Collection. The Center for Puerto Rican Studies Library and Archives. Hunter College, CUNY.

NOT THE TIME TO STAY

CHARACTERS
JAIME, a man
MONCHO, his father
HILDA/MOTHER, Jaime's wife as well as Jaime's mother (both characters played by the same actress)
JAIME'S MIRROR IMAGE

The stage is in total darkness. The sound that saturates the space, much before the action begins, is a mix of electronic music, the sound of glass breaking, the soft melody of a flute, a persistent clock alarm, and music that suggests either the creation or the destruction of the world, such as Olivier Messiaen's "Et Exspecto Resurrectionem Mortuorum." Its progression moves from weak to solemn, to monstrous, to impossible. We are witness to the sounds of a nightmare. We hear the clock alarm one last time in the overture. At the same time, the man sleeping on the bed in the middle of the stage sits up under a light that blinds him, as if a horrible nightmare haunted him. The man, JAIME, wipes his face with his hands and looks around, bewildered. The clock alarm keeps going. JAIME turns it off with a sudden move. Meanwhile, to the right of the audience, a light blue light shines upon the enormous frame of a mirror, in which the man will be able to look at himself in full length. The mirror (simply, a hollow frame) is suspended sideways so that the audience is able to see both the man and his image.

JAIME realizes the mirror has lightened up. He moves towards it with a slow pace, full of curiosity, lost in thought. While he walks towards the mirror, his image, on the other side, moves towards him at the same rhythm, copying his movements. Once they are face to face, JAIME will extend his arms so that the palms of his hands and those of his image are joined together. Following this, he tries to approach his image sexually, in a sort of almost indiscernible dance, or an almost religious ritual. Finally, his lips join those of his image in a nervous and almost desperate kiss.

From the moment JAIME turns off the clock alarm to the kiss, an increasing tension has been established through electronic music.

HILDA
No one's stopping me now, Jaime. Its 3:10, not the time to stay. (*Looking a bit annoyed.*) Where's my umbrella?

Her voice has come from the other side of the stage (to the left of the audience), which is illuminated by a yellowish light that represents the woman's voice. The light on the mirror disappeared the precise moment the woman interrupts the previous scene with the intensity of her voice. On stage, we only see the dishevelled woman, who has a half-

smoked cigarette on her nervous hand. The woman's attire does not give away her age. Her appearance is sufficiently vague as to represent either a long-suffering young woman or a middle-aged woman who still looks young.

HILDA *stops looking*
Repeat, repeat, repeat is all I do lately. There's no salvaging our relationship. We talk, and talk, and talk, to make it to the same point again. You and I are too old already to play this game. We're not eighteen. Look at my face. Look at the hands I have left. I look like a whore from a Mexican film. Next thing you know I'll be singing a *bolero* with a wineglass on my hand. I'm up to here (*touching her brow*) with being cooped up in the house. I have the right to do myself up and be beautiful. How old am I? What would I know! Twenty-five, thirty, thirty-five... But I can still light a fire. If only I weren't a decent woman. But I'm respectful. I'm very catholic, damn it! (*Pauses to change her bitter attitude into a more sarcastic one*). There's a letter for you, from your mother, the goody two-shoes, who thinks she's better than the rest of us. (*Mocking her in-law's voice.*) "My son, that woman is no good for you. You know what they say around town? That she's not a virgin. You've studied. You can do better than that!" (*Violently now.*) Of course I wasn't a virgin. They'd popped my cherry when I was thirteen (*pauses, reflects briefly*), no, fourteen. But you knew that, Jaime. I never denied anything to you. You already knew all of my history when we ran away together, and you still said you loved me. Jaime, what has happened between us? What happened to us?

HILDA takes JAIME's hand. He's just made it to where she is. To the left of the audience, there are two white buckets, different in size. One acts as a dinning table, the other one as a chair. We can hear the theme played by the flute while she asks the questions. It will also serve as a transition to Jaime's following phrase. The yellow light turns into a bright white.

JAIME
Mom, I told you it's nothing. Nothing's going on.

MOTHER *brushing his hair with her hands*
Something's going on. Those angry outbursts, the bad manners, that's not your usual self.

JAIME
He started it. Why does he have to ask those questions? He knows my point of view in those matters.

MOTHER
He does, he does. But you are younger and have to do your bit. Whenever your father brings those up, keep quiet to avoid arguments. He is an ill man. You know the doctor has forbid him to get all upset because it gets his ulcer going, and it's not that big a

leap to go from an ulcer to stomach cancer.

JAIME
Why are you defending him now? You've bad-mouthed him yourself, complaining day and night about how much he's made you suffer.

MOTHER
But that's different. I'm his wife. He's your father and you have to respect him. It's amongst God's ten commandments: "Honor thy father and thy mother."

JAIME
And what does "Honor thy father and thy mother" mean? To hand over your whole life to them and your whole future so that they can prolong their frustrations through their children?

MOTHER
But take into consideration that your father is ill.

JAIME *in a sarcastic tone*
Ill? That has been his excuse to get what he wants, all the time. A corpse... a living death. And who the fuck's alive in this house?

MOTHER *trying to silence his protests with overt motherly tenderness*
Son, son, don't speak that way. God is going to punish you.

JAIME *exasperated*
Fuck God!

MOTHER lifts her gaze in a solemn demeanour, as if interfering for her son before God.

MOTHER
You've changed so much, my son! You weren't like this as a child. You were so quiet and respectful. You went to confession and took your communion every Sunday. And you even thought of becoming a priest! (*Changing her tone into one of acceptance.*) Well, thank God I can't complain. You were always a perfect child, but even so, a mother suffers and does not mind about sacrificing her life for that of her children. That's our mission on Earth. I don't want anything for myself. A dress and a pair of shoes are enough for me; I've been poor all of my life. But I want everything for my children, God willing. You'll realize all I've sacrificed for you one day. I've rather fed you than myself.

JAIME

The problem is that you refuse to accept that I am not a child anymore.

MOTHER

But don't you understand? You are my only child. Why did you have to grow up? What for did you learn to walk on your own, to run errands? You don't need me anymore. I'm a useless old rag. (*Firm and proud.*) Your damn father... He always thought himself to be single. Always hanging out with his friends, being irresponsible. (*Forcing her emotions.*) The many sleepless nights I spent with you in my arms! And he'd come home at the break of dawn, drunk, and get into bed with us. How disgusting! Smelling of rum and women, sweat and cigarettes. Such hard and cold hands! What a torture his scorching body was! I'd hold back my tears and clench my jaw. You know what I was? A tool he left at home, to use only when he wanted to unload his *macho* brutality. One night he even tried to kill you because I refused to take you out of our bed and put you on the crib by yourself. You needed me so much then. Not now.

JAIME

Hilda, you are my wife. You don't have to leave the house to go work. What I make is enough to eat and live. A woman's place is her home.

HILDA

Yes, but I get bored within these four walls. I'm not the kind of woman who stays home all day listening to radio soap operas. If at least we had children... In the beginning, it was all different because it was all new. We loved each other. We understood each other. But now, no matter how much we talk, we don't get each other.

JAIME

Are you ready?

HILDA *surprised*

For what?

JAIME

We're going out.

HILDA

But don't you have work today?

JAIME

No, I took the day off to be with you.

HILDA
But we spend time together every night. You'll lose your job!

JAIME
Even so. I miss you when I go to work. I picture you here, by yourself, bored, and I feel like quitting everything and coming back home.

HILDA
The same thing happens to me. I start doing my house chores and I think about the night before, and all the nice things you say to me, and all our plans to move to a new neighbourhood, and have a house made out of cement, with its own garage and an ornamental iron fence. I look at last night's dirty sheets, the whole of the bed, and I feel it warm still.

JAIME *kisses her*
Should we go out? It's Friday, and Fridays were not meant to be working days.

HILDA *flirty*
And what were they meant for?

JAIME looks at her lustfully and pulls her by the arm towards the bed.

JAIME
Come to bed and I'll show you.

HILDA
No, no, no. I have to fix myself up if we're going out.

JAIME *berating her sweetly*
Would you like a hammer and nails to fix yourself? Mrs, you don't have to beautify yourself for anyone.

HILDA
Of course I do. A woman must keep her good looks. Otherwise, her husband will go looking for good looks somewhere else.

JAIME
You don't have to worry about me because you got me head over heels.

HILDA pushes him playfully. They laugh and celebrate his comment. The Messiaen-like music begins to take over the environment, and will stay in the background during the dialogue that follows. In it, the characters seem to be speaking to each other but their movements do not correspond to what they are saying.

JAIME
Yes, yes. Can you see the pictures came out too dark?

HILDA
It needs more salt. My mom used to pour lemon juice on the meat. It gives it a different taste.

JAIME
Flowers were raining over the fire.

HILDA
What did the forecast say?

JAIME
There are rulers that are more than twelve inches long.

HILDA
The sea breeze also whets the appetite.

JAIME
It's impossible for me to get it up on Fridays.

HILDA
Like that, like that. Are you cumming?

JAIME
I can't. I don't love you anymore.

HILDA
I know. My teats are saggy, my belly is wrinkly, my thighs full of varicose veins. My walls have dilated. Jaime, you forget I am about thirty years old and God knows how much time I have left. What do I do?

JAIME
It's not that. The body is beyond this. Look, right now I can't touch you because you are over there. (*He stretches his hand to touch her and can't reach her.*) If your body were to extinguish, there wouldn't be a trace of you.

HILDA
It's not my body? Damn it! What the fuck is this? What else can a woman give to a man? That is her natural and normal purpose. Each one of us has to perform our role in life. You can't demand more than that from me. That's all I have, all I was taught to do.

JAIME *entirely in some other world*
That's what I mean. Did someone call me?

HILDA doesn't reply.

JAIME *insistently*
Did someone call me?

MOTHER
There isn't much, really. I'm making a codfish soup. Your father didn't leave any money for us this week. The little I made ironing I gave to you so that you could buy some clothes. What else do you want?

JAIME *with an annoyed face*
Mom, I don't...

HILDA *interrupts him*
I know you don't like it, but we are poor and you have to get used to it. Life is hard, but we must accept God's will. There are some sweet potatoes, too. You like sweet potatoes.

There is a brief pause after which some sobs escape her. HILDA cries harder until she loses control.

MONCHO
And what's wrong with you now?

MOTHER
Ay, Moncho. Jaime left at ten last night and he still hasn't come back. I think something's happened to the kid. May God watch over him. I'm going crazy. I don't know what to do anymore. He's never spent a night out of his home...

MONCHO
Don't you worry, woman. Stop the whining. He's probably gone to San Juan to get some whore to pop his cherry. And well done, because he's old enough already. It's time for him to break off your damn bosom.

MOTHER *unsettled*

Moncho, even God can't forgive you. How can you be so cruel in a moment like this? I'm telling you Jaime wouldn't dare spend the night out of his home. He's just a kid.

MONCHO *yelling*

Woman, stop that shit. You're driving me crazy with your hogwash.

MOTHER

Moncho, call the police. Do something. I am just a woman. Men deal with these kinds of things.

MONCHO

Look, I'm leaving this house before I lose my patience and beat you up.

MOTHER *aggressive*

You never wanted him. You always treated him as if he were a dog. God will punish you for the bad life you've given us. Divine justice will make sure to put everything in its place. Leave. I'll go to the police station myself; I'll identify the body if necessary. My poor son. (*Makes the sign of the holy cross.*) May God have him in His glory.

MONCHO *not paying attention to his wife*

Your son is spoiled. You remember the other day? How he raised his voice at me when we were talking politics? Piece of shit like that, what does he know about politics? What does he know about the times when we were so poor we'd gnaw on each other? To talk to me about independence...

MOTHER

Moncho, it's just that youngsters can't see how much we've progressed in these last few years, to the point of becoming "the showcase of the Caribbean." They can't see that years ago these roads, these fancy buildings, the post offices with the pretty flags did not exist. And most importantly, they can't appreciate the peace we've always had in this country. When have we seen blood on our streets? We are pacifists and will remain so – God and the Holly Church willing.

MONCHO

Yes, but they want to fuck everything up with their patriotism and their freedom. What more freedom than the one we have? We can say whatever we feel like in this country without fearing we'll go to jail. You know what's happening? That he's hanging out with communists at that university, and forgets about the decency he's been taught at home. All he needs is three good punches to get all that shit about freedom out of his system, and start behaving properly. Reckless kid.

MOTHER *startled*
Shhh, here he comes.

MONCHO
And why do you shush me? Here, I can say whatever the fuck I want.

MOTHER and MONCHO's eyes follow JAIME's movements. He has come in and sat down.

MONCHO
Where were you? (*Pauses.*) Hey, I asked you a question. You think because you're going to university you're better than your father and mother? You're playing dumb now? Don't forget you wouldn't be were you are if it weren't for us, you lazy bum. Know what you should do? Get a job.

MOTHER
Moncho, don't talk like that. Poor thing just got home. God knows what happened to him.

MONCHO
And how do you want me to talk? Lazy bum here thinks he's the boss of him. Your mother didn't sleep all night, and you show yourself home at this time, safe and sound, not a scratch, and a fresh face.

MOTHER
Son, what happened to you? Where were you? I was dead worried. (*She insists, teary-eyed, taking him by the shoulders.*) What happened? Tell me. Where were you?

JAIME
In San Juan, fucking some whore.

MOTHER laughs out loud, like a girl full of enthusiasm. JAIME is infected by her laugh.

JAIME *laughing still*
If only you had seen my mother's face to my reply.

HILDA
I can imagine. What did she do then?

JAIME
She slapped me so hard my teeth felt loose. But the next day, I went to San Juan again.

HILDA
And your father?

JAIME
I don't know. Maybe he's dead.

HILDA
Dead? Dead? How many times?

JAIME *thinks, calculates*
I think just once.

HILDA laughs out loud again, hugging and kissing him in a childish manner. When she recovers her seriousness she gets melancholic.

HILDA
How many children you think we'll have?

JAIME *distracted*
Don't know. Many.

HILDA
I don't want to raise my children the way I was raised. You know, always being shouted to, getting hit with the belt. I think if one's going to grow up to be decent, one will be it, no need to beat one up. (*Trying to get Jaime's attention.*) You should know a lot about that, with what you've studied at university.

JAIME
That has nothing to do with studying. But you're right.

HILDA
Jaime, I wish I had studied like you. Go to university, if possible, you know. Because sometimes I fear you.

JAIME
How silly! Why do you fear me?

HILDA
Because I don't understand you. Sometimes we're together and it seems like your mind is somewhere far away, lost in another world I don't know of. When we're in bed, that's different, because there we don't talk. But out of bed, I lose you. You hold a mystery within that worries me, and I think it's that you know things I can't understand. I know you love me, but sometimes I think you'll leave me all alone one day, and run off with a lettered woman.

JAIME
The things you say! That has nothing to do with studying. What time is it?

HILDA *avoiding the question*
I told him I didn't want that dress three times. It's tight at the waistline.

JAIME *raising his voice*
What time is it?

HILDA *insists on avoiding the question*
How many times do you want me to tell you I won't be paying that bill? You can take the encyclopaedia back if you want. Encyclopaedias, encyclopaedias, for what? There are no school-aged children here that could use them.

JAIME *at the point of desperation*
What time is it?

HILDA
This day is fucked up. It's been drizzling all day, and it's not that wet, but it's not that dry either. (*Searching.*) Where is my umbrella?

JAIME *violently*
What time is it?

HILDA *stares at him realizing she can't avoid the question anymore*
Yes, he was here almost all afternoon waiting for you.

JAIME *visibly interested*
And what did he say? How is he?

HILDA
Like always. He said he was leaving for New York. Where is New York? Everybody's leaving for New York. What's in New York? Must be a beautiful city where all your

problems get solved. But it seems to me people don't go to New York looking for something, but running away from something. What's everyone running away from, Jaime? Why don't they stay and solve their problems here?

JAIME *taken aback*
He's leaving for New York? (*He sits down.*)

HILDA
I wonder what that man is up to.

JAIME
What do you mean?

HILDA
Don't know. He's so quiet and mysterious. Barely talks. Why does he look for you so often?

JAIME
For the same reason I look for him. We're friends. He's always offered to help whenever I've been on a tight spot.

We hear the flute's music theme for a while.

MOTHER
Son, your friend came here looking for you. What's his name?

JAIME
Jaime, his name is Jaime, like me.

MOTHER
That's the one. He said he needed to talk to you urgently, but...

JAIME hastily gets up, cutting off his mother's words.

MOTHER *calling him*
Jaime, where are you going?

JAIME
To his house, to see what he wants.

MOTHER
I forbid you to go.

JAIME *takes it as a joke*
What are you saying?

MOTHER
I'm saying, don't go looking for him. I don't like that kid. Your friendship gives people
something to talk about. People talk...

JAIME
Are you crazy? People can go to hell!

MOTHER *looking imposing and determined*
I'd rather kill my son with my own hands than have him turn out to be a faggot.

*JAIME sweetly puts his arms around her neck and lays a solemn kiss on her forehead.
We hear the clock alarm as the bed lights up. He runs to turn it off and begins to laugh
uncontrollably. The light on the dinning room area has disappeared; there is light only
over the bed. Once JAIME turns off the clock alarm, the blue light on the mirror area
returns. JAIME walks, drawn by the mirror, and meets his image. They look at each
other attentively. Between them there is an air of happiness, a silence full of expecta-
tion. They brake into a nervous laugh as a result of their unsuccessful search for words
to communicate.*

JAIME
They tell me you're leaving.

IMAGE
Yes.

JAIME
What about me? What do I do?

IMAGE
What do you mean, *what do you do?*

JAIME
I mean, who will I talk to? One gets lonely. It's hard to be out here without anyone
who understands.

IMAGE *smiling*

Sometimes even I don't understand you. The times when we were able to guess what each other was thinking are gone. We can't race each other playing *chasey* around the neighbourhood streets anymore. We can't escape to the river to bathe naked and eat guavas either. The policeman's daughter is now too old to bribe her with sweets so that she comes with us to that spot beneath the house and do thingies.

JAIME

We can't go behind the outhouse near the ranch to jerk off and see whose gets farther either.

IMAGE

Look at these grown bodies. They've lost their blonde fuzz. Now they have hard muscles, tense backbones that emanate a morbid heat. We can't exchange them anymore because they are different.

MOTHER'S VOICE

(*While she speaks, JAIME and his IMAGE remain still.*) Jaime, dinner is served. Where are you? Open that door. There you are, as always, standing in front of the mirror. Come on, get here. Men shouldn't be looking in the mirror so much anyway.

JAIME

Sometimes, when I look in the mirror, I feel like I'm spying on a stranger. You have my eyes, my mouth, my chest, the curve on my back, my sex. You are the reflection of all those things. And yet I feel you have an existence of your own. Sometimes I undress in front of the mirror and talk to myself, believing I reply to myself from the inside. When I touch your body, it's not my body I touch. The stubble on your beard hurts me.

IMAGE

It would have been easier if you'd been able to cross into this mirror. But what can I do, an image against its original? Without you, where would I be? Only you can make our encounter happen. Come in, come in. You're coming to me more often each time, but you stay on the other side, covered in sweat and feat. Come in, enter.

JAIME *desperate*

There's more glass in the world each time. Words are no good to get to people. There is too much dead weight over my body. I'm buried under bibles and alphabets. It's not water what rains over me; it's questions that make no sense and have no answer.

IMAGE

I follow you, I mimic you, I duplicate you, I multiply you in my efforts to prevent your death. But that's all that's within my reach. You are on the other side, with your wife, like sardines jumping on a net, under what's left of dusk. You're with her but without you. Now, you're no more than a long silence brought about by itself.

JAIME
I can communicate with you.

IMAGE
Because you talk to me through the body and body language is the only comprehensible one, our last resort. It is the foundation for all of our love, understanding, tolerance, our frustration. The body we can't get rid of despite how much we scourge it. My denial is your self-destruction.

JAIME *in an effort to escape the tension*
Huy, how serious! You know, if our lives were represented in a novel, or a play, or something of the like, you'd be the devil, you'd have two little horns, a trident, a deafening laugh, and would be surrounded by red smoke.

IMAGE
And you'd be the good soul, debating yourself between the good and the bad.

They both laugh.

JAIME *returning to a serious tone*
But I can't tell her. I can't confess to her that when I look at myself in the mirror there's an image that mimics what I do. She wouldn't understand me. It's you who exists, me who copies your movements, your words. It's you who ties me to the mirror and makes me move inward. (*Begging.*) Don't leave me now.

IMAGE
We haven't been able to kill the kids we were. Our blood pact constantly renews itself. Did you bring the razor?

JAIME
Yes, here it is. We must make a pact: to never part from each other. (*He carries out his words.*) Small cuts on the index fingers. Bloods are mixing. Eyes are fixed on the hands joined by blood. Let's take our fingers to our mouths and drink our mixed blood. (*Uncomfortable.*) It's hot. Damn heat! (*Suddenly in fear.*) The Earth will split in two and will swallow us whole. We'll be struck by lightning.

IMAGE
Jaime, do you think this is sacrilegious? Should it come up in confession on Sunday?

JAIME
I don't think so. The indigenous did it. Plus, there are so many other means of punishment...

IMAGE
I stayed still in the middle of the meadow, with the taste of fresh blood on my hot tongue and lightning never came.

JAIME
Lightning never came. Maybe we're waiting for a sort of punishment that does not exist. We should punish ourselves.

The IMAGE turns his back to JAIME. JAIME whips him in a violent and poetic panto-mime. The IMAGE does the same him to JAIME. They both end up taking deep breaths.

IMAGE
Do you feel better now?

JAIME nods.

IMAGE
Me too.

JAIME
People say I'm crazy, that what I say makes no sense. And yet it all seems so clear to me. Everything I say betrays me, but much of what I do defines me.

HILDA'S VOICE
I've tried to figure out what makes us different and I've learned that we're all different; we're all unique.

JAIME *answers to her voice in the distance*
It's not true! I don't know anything.

MOTHER'S VOICE
Jaime, get off the street. Leave the bike and get into the house.

JAIME
But I just went out...

MOTHER
I've said to get in. I don't want any arguing. That damn bike is a threat. I have no idea why your damn godfather bought you that crap.

JAIME
Mom, let me stay out a little bit longer.

MOTHER
Don't make me say it again: get in the house. Don't you understand I'm by myself? Do you want me to die here all by myself and be found because of the stink? *Ay, my lord!* Why do we raise our children and sacrifice for them? I am sick. (*In a victimized tone.*) Be a bit considerate to your mother. (*Developing energy all of a sudden.*) Who's out there with you? Those voices, Jaime, who are you talking to? To that little friend of yours? I've told you I don't want to see you with him.

JAIME
I'm coming, Mom. I'm coming now.

JAIME composes himself and takes one last look at the image to then run towards his mother's voice. Light comes on over the dining room, while the mirror area darkens. Electronic music aids the transition. HILDA is impatiently pacing up and down the dining room.

HILDA
Why are you asking me to stay? This is all absurd. You're behaving like a child. (Reacting violently to a new plea for her to stay.) I'm telling you I'm leaving! I'm fed up with this house and the nonsense you talk about while you shower. Take yesterday for example: "I twisted my ankle trying to figure out our monthly bills."

JAIME *shocked and sceptical*
You're not leaving. You're kidding.

HILDA *astonished, gives him a cold look*
Let me tell you it is 3:25, not the time to stay.

JAIME caresses her hair and eventually grabs her hand to caress it, with some apprehension. From here on to the end of their litany, the light moves very slowly over the bed.

HILDA *rescuing her hand from his caress*
It's 12:30... Three years. Three years... These are not toys or leaves, and they won't be. You think I don't know? Can't you see how the future exploded inside of me...?

The flute's theme serves as the background for the narration of this episode in HILDA's childhood.

HILDA

When I was little, I was terrified of New Year's Eve parties. I couldn't stand the noise of the firecrackers. The guys would follow me and throw them at my feet. I'd run and yell, like a madwoman, and that'd make them follow me even more. Now I feel like everything I ever dreamed of exploded in my head, just like a firecracker.

JAIME *as in another dimension*
Hilda, dump that clock. Get rid of it.

HILDA
I can't. It was a birthday gift.

JAIME *with a childish interest*
Who gave it to you?

HILDA
You did, two years ago. But don't worry. It doesn't work anymore.

JAIME
Yes, I understand.

HILDA *reacting against the intimacy established through the dialogue*
Do not stop me. You see those steps scattered on the floor? I have to follow them.

JAIME *taking her by the shoulders, non-violently*
You're not leaving.

HILDA
What the hell do you want me to do? To stay and fill my life with bricks? To get my mouth down to your sex every night to give you the freedom to walk outside yourself and over everything else?

JAIME
I'd like to have a dog. Mom, they offered me a dog...

MOTHER *categorically*
No!

JAIME
Black and white, this small.

MOTHER
No!

JAIME
A pure breed.

MOTHER
No! Don't you bring any animals in here. I don't want any dog shitting around the house, and I know you're not prepared to clean the shit. If you show up with a dog here I'll kick you both out. *Ay, Herod, why didn't you take this one along with all the other children?*

JAIME
But I can leave him outside.

MOTHER *condescending*
Here you go (*Hands him money.*). Go to the movies and forget about the dog.

JAIME
But I don't want to go to the movies. I prefer the dog.

MOTHER
Take it before you end up without the dog and the money.

JAIME takes the money and is about to leave. We hear HILDA's laugh again.

HILDA *laughing sweetly*
If only you were always like this, like a child, how different would things be! But sometimes you get so big. Sometimes you are a brilliant erection.

HILDA *puts her hands over his sex and says, as if saying a litany:*
That over there is a bed

JAIME
That waits for us

HILDA
I am a woman

JAIME
That waits

HILDA
You are a tree

JAIME
That waits

HILDA
Mystery

JAIME
That waits

HILDA
That over there is a car

JAIME
That waits for us

HILDA
There are two spoons on the bed

JAIME
They wait for us

HILDA
Children are waiting behind each orgasm

JAIME
They wait for us

HILDA
That over there is life

JAIME
That waits for us

HILDA
That over there is us

JAIME
Waiting for ourselves

HILDA takes him by the hand. JAIME lets her lead him to the bed, which, at this point, is fully illuminated. Now next to the bed, HILDA bares her breasts.

HILDA *offering her breasts to him*
You're hungry. Suck here, my love, my baby boy.

JAIME refuses with a childish shake of the head.

JAIME
Mom, nothing's going on. I'm fine.

MOTHER
Suck, my son. I know you're hungry.

JAIME starts crying and she comforts him with motherly caresses.

JAIME *while crying*
Where is Dad? He promised we'd go fishing today.

JAIME throws himself on the bed and from then on he adopts MONCHO's personality.

MOTHER *furious, fixing her dress*
You ask me?! As if I knew his whereabouts!

MOTHER turns abruptly to talk to an imaginary Jaime.

MOTHER *taking her index finger to her lips*
Shhhhhh! Go play outside; your father's asleep. (*Pauses*) Do not contradict me, pick everything up and go outside.

MOTHER turns abruptly to verbally attack her husband, who's lying on the bed.

MOTHER *with her hands lying on her hips*
You got a good thing going! Spending all night out, coming home at dawn to take a rest from the parties.

MONCHO
Shut up, woman. You're always nagging me. I don't feel good today. Leave me alone

MOTHER
You want me to leave you alone while we starve? How long has it been since you last gave us a penny?

MONCHO
Things are bad. What about the money you make ironing?

MOTHER *sarcastically*
I give it to the poor.

MONCHO *not really paying attention*
Who won at the races? (*With satisfaction*) Horse races will be my ruin or my salvation.

MOTHER
I played a ticket, but it fell through by the second race. I've no luck at races. I prefer the lottery. Did you know Juana, the butcher, won at the numbers? (*Impressed*) She made a hundred bucks!

MONCHO *uninterested*
I'm glad for her and her team of anaemic kids.

There is an unending silence. MONCHO seems worried.

MONCHO
I'm leaving tomorrow.

MOTHER *avoiding to confront the news*
I've had this terrible headache since yesterday. It's killing me. Must be my nerves.

MONCHO
I'm leaving tomorrow. I already have the ticket. I didn't want to leave without telling you.

MOTHER
I'm nauseous. First thing tomorrow, I'll make an appointment at the free clinic. I think I won't last long.

The silence returns. He repeats the question with his eyes. She understands she can't avoid it any longer.

MOTHER
That decision all of a sudden?

MONCHO
It's not sudden. I've been thinking about it for a long time. I'm sick of all this. I want a change. There's more of a future for me in New York. Money rains over there. I could come back to the island in a couple of years and set up my own barbershop. I'm tired of working for other people. From now on, I want to be my own boss.

MOTHER
Do you want me to pack your bags?

MONCHO
Just one. As soon as I'm all set up I'll send for you. By then, Jaime will know how to fend for himself.

MOTHER
Do you want me to iron your white shirts or should I take them to the laundry?

MONCHO
There's no time for that. I leave tomorrow morning.

The flute's theme emerges from a deep and solid silence.

MOTHER
Jaime, don't leave. Don't grow up. You're the one thing I have left ever since your father died.

JAIME *who has recovered his identity upon listening the flute's theme*
My father is not dead.

MOTHER
Yes, he is. He abandoned us. But I prefer to think that bastard is dead. You're my only son. The one thing I have left.

JAIME
Mom, I love Hilda. I'm taking her with me.

MOTHER
My son, that woman is no good for you. You know what they say around town? That she's not a virgin. You've studied. You can do better than that.

JAIME
That has nothing to do with studying. I'm leaving with her.

MOTHER
Everybody leaves: Moncho, you. Why do you leave me alone? Where are you going? Where is New York? What's in New York?

JAIME *pointing north*
Do you see that yellow light shining in the distance? (*She nods.*) That's New York. Seduced by the light, moths go towards it. Once they get too close, their wings burn and they can't come back. Dad will never come back. He has nothing to look for in this breeding ground for mosquitoes. Family always belongs to the past. Children are a future of their own, independent, little to do with their parents.

MOTHER *abruptly letting go of Jaime*
Don't leave with that whore!

JAIME begins to walk back, his eyes always set on his mother's face. While he disappears into the darkness outside the luminous circle around the bed, she takes her hands to her neck to protect herself.

MOTHER *yelling*
Jaime, you're crazy. I am your mother. No, Jaime, no, no.

Her last words are labored. She falls on the bed. The clock alarm goes off for some time. Its sound disappears so that we can hear the sound of the flute. The dining room is illuminated. We hear JAIME and HILDA's laughs, during happier times in their relationship. Jaime is sitting at the dinner table, reading a letter. The VOICE of the IMAGE reads the texts.

VOICE of the IMAGE

Dear friend,

It's been very difficult for me to adapt to this city, but lately, I've understood its allure. After spending so much time in this enormous circus, it would be impossible for me to go back to the narrowness of my town. I would drown in people's familiar ways. Nobody knows me here, nobody looks for me, and yet they all understand me, no words needed, because we all share an almost religious isolation. Neither life or death are celebrations here.

A third of me is here, working, diminishing, so that life can go on over there, so that you live. I am the fertilizer, the ashes that long await to rise again. The time of the rain that will make us repeat the cycle is coming. I have already found what I was looking for, thus, you don't exist.

The actor (JAIME) looks at the audience, puzzled.

MOTHER
Jaime, don't leave. I don't want to die alone.

JAIME
Everybody dies alone, and is born alone.

HILDA
If you see me over there, promise me you'll recognize me.

JAIME
I can't promise such things. I'm going into the unknown. (*Calling out loudly*) Jaime!

The IMAGE, who is lying on the bed in the middle of the stage wakes up upon hearing its name. It moves towards the mirror, calling itself. It enters it, calling on the rest of the characters, who do not answer or show up. It goes back to the bed to find JAIME on it, waking from a deep sleep. They smile. JAIME extends his hands to draw the IMAGE towards him. The IMAGE lets itself be brought to the bed as the lights fade out very slowly.

END OF PLAY

CALL MY NUMBER (1977)

A dramatic monologue based on poems and letters by Julia de Burgos

CHARACTERS
ACTRESS, Julia 1
DANCER, Julia 2
HE, male dancer

A note from director Víctor Fragoso:

Born in the town of Carolina, Puerto Rico, during one of the most difficult periods of the island, Julia de Burgos grew up in close contact with nature. Her trees and her river, birds and butterflies, flowers and fruits, are the elements that form "her" world, the poetic world that the woman superimposes on a harsh, often ugly, urban reality. Her main preoccupation is that of the artist in our century: the debate between the personal search and our responsibility to others. She fluctuates, immersed at times in her own, undefinable agony; at others, identified with the suffering of the working masses of the world, and specifically those who struggle for the liberation of Puerto Rico. Her sensitivity allows her to analyse in depth the situations she encounters. Often, out of her analysis, predictions are derived. Strangely, many of the things she wrote in her poems became realities later on. She amazes everyone with her intelligence, and shocks the world around her with unexpected actions that often clash with the rules of the society in which she has to live. She is athletic and adventurous, bold and enthusiastic. In her early twenties, she falls in love with a Dominican left-wing intellectual during his visit to Puerto Rico. Her short lived marriage, sometime before, gives way to a new period of exuberant passion, drifting from anguish to ecstasy with fierce energy. In 1940, she follows him, without much analysis, to New York. After a short period of excitement and exploration, the city becomes an immense machine that slowly devours her. Her lover leaves for Cuba. She is supposed to follow him shortly. Her last months in New York, and her trip to Florida, where she was to board the ship that would take her to her lover, were hard to bear. On the bus to Miami she had a nervous breakdown.

Cuba is a land of promise for her. She is again, next to her loved one, discovering a country she admired, a land so similar to her own. Her first book had been well received by the critics in Puerto Rico. She was now working on a new one, under the impulse of her feelings for her lover, and of the world she was now discovering, guided by him. Following him, she became dependent. He presented her with a contradictory reality: he seemed to enjoy being with her, and making plans for the future, but he hid her from friends because his family opposed the relationship. Her life takes a new tragic turn when she discovered that, once the obstacles for their relationship were gone, he still did not want to commit himself to her. One day he brings her a ticket to

New York. She is to leave the same afternoon. She would not go back to Puerto Rico because she did not want to face "certain people and situations that she had left behind." In 1942, she is back in New York, alone and often desperate. She marries briefly and goes to live in Washington with her husband, but they cannot tolerate the isolation, and decide to return to New York. She is now drinking heavily. Around 1948, she becomes seriously ill; she has developed an infection of the vocal chords, apparently a rare disease that makes her an easy guinea pig for doctors and medical students, who surround her bed when she least expect it. In her anguish, sometimes she rebels against the nurses, and leaves her bed, but she is subdued and punished, forced to stay in bed all day, and threatened to be released even when she has nowhere to go. In June 1953, a month before her death, she writes one of the last letters to her sister. She has escaped from the hospital, and is writing from the bridge that connects Welfare Island to the mainland. She is wearing a worn out hospital robe. She knows death is close. They are going to release her from the hospital soon. She asks for a couple of dollars to buy soap and toothpaste. Shortly after, she is released from the hospital. Before going to another sister's house, where she is supposed to stay until she is back on her feet, she stays with a relative in Brooklyn. From there, she leaves for her sister's house. She never arrived. She was found dead near 105th Street and Fifth Avenue, without a purse or any kind of identification. The autopsy revealed that she had died of pneumonia. Weeks later her body was identified by her relatives, and taken back to her homeland, where she was received and paid homage as a great poet.

Call my number *is the title of one of de Burgos most anguished poems. Exhausted, her aspirations now shattered, she finds no sense in living. Death approaches slowly, not fast enough for her. She sees it approaching inexorably, and faces it defiantly, crying: "Call my number / What are they waiting for / What else do they want of me?" Starting from the moment in which she is writing her last letter to her sister, jumping briefly to the poem that she wrote (in English) in the Goldwater Memorial Hospital, Julia searches in her memory for loved images: her childhood, her mother, the hills of her hometown, the river along which she played, in which she bathed as an adolescent and hard erotic discoveries. Through the monologue, she reviews her life, faces herself, unfolds, and wins, through her poetic works, the battle that she apparently lost in real life. At the end, she transcends death, knowing that she will remain through her words: "Am I dead? Am I alive? Present! Here! Present!" The dancer is her other self, her little sister, her mother, and images of other women. The play is, therefore, a dialogue in which words are answered with movement, or become one with movement, or are highlighted by movement. The male dancer is the man: all men, and the special man in which she deposits her sense of self for a brief and painful moment. The audience is her sister, to whom all the letters are addressed, and society, against which she rebels at times. The parachute at center stage transforms by means of pulleys and lights to create different spaces and structures. The light is condensed, and often traps her in certain spaces; it is the instrument with which the outsiders probe her inner world; it falls at awkward angles.*

SCENE 1.

Total darkness. The electronic music fills the space and increases steadily. Gradual light over the figure of a woman (ACTRESS – JULIA 1), who is standing on the bridge that connects Welfare Island with the mainland. She has escaped from the hospital to walk a little and take some fresh air. She is mortally ill and knows it.

ACTRESS

"I write to you from the island's bridge, where I've escaped to from all the doctors for a few minutes. It's all enclosed on my floor. Temperature is set at 75. I need fresh air. I'm only wearing a hospital gown. I discovered a post from which I could send you this brief letter before the nurses come to take me back to bed."

As light dims on the actress, the figure of DANCER – JULIA 2 gradually appears, sitting on the stoop of a building. It is July. DANCER has been walking aimlessly. She has terminal pneumonia. She can hardly breathe. Her final moment is near. She hears her own voice (recorded) saying one of her final poems. She makes an effort to get up and continue walking. ACTRESS watches her and, in an effort to delay death, she calls on the DANCER to find support in images of childhood, her homeland, and love.

Voice of ACTRESS (recorded)
"It has to come from here,[1]
Right this instant,
My cry into the world.

Life was somewhere forgotten
And sought refuge in depths of tears
And sorrows
Over this vast empire of solitude
And darkness.
Where is the voice of freedom,
Freedom to laugh,
To move
Without the heavy phantom of despair?
Where is the form of beauty
Unshaken in its veil, simple and pure?"

---

[1] "Farewell from Welfare Island." Fragoso has edited most poems for brevity and theme.

The DANCER reacts to the call to live of the ACTRESS by bringing out the beautiful poetic world that covers despair and loneliness through her dance.

ACTRESS
Your shadowless spring waters will be present within you.[2]
You will be on the branches of the entire world.
Let me sing to you like when you were mine
Under the fresh drizzle of the first downpour.

Let me sing to you like when you were mine,
My wild little sister, like when we would climb
The star that'd come to dream of loneliness
Amongst our pupils, distilled by love.

Let me sing to you like when you were mine
And there was peace in the silence of my deep wave
And there was peace in the distance between your name and mine
And there was peace in the whimper of the death that waits.

Your shadowless spring waters will be present within you...
You will be on the branches of my entire world
And every single star will come down all singing
That song about space sheltered by the river.

In her attempt to bring the DANCER back to life, the ACTRESS conjures the image of the river, which is one of the leit motifs of the poetic world of Julia de Burgos. The DANCER picks up the river from the back of the earth, and drinks it, wraps it around her body, and flies with it in her dreams. During the final verse of the river poem, the DANCER disappears. The ACTRESS is alone. Out of the image of the river emerges the image of her mother (DANCER).

ACTRESS
Great Loíza River! Elongate on my spirit[3]
Letting my soul adrift amongst your streams,
So I can find the fountain that took you away as a child
And in its maddened impulse returned you to your path.
Coil yourself on my lips and let me drink from you

---

2 "Para Julia de Burgos."

3 "Río Grande de Loíza."

So that for a brief moment I feel that you are mine
Conceal you from the world, and in yourself conceal you
To hear astonished voices escaping the wind's mouth
Descend just for a moment from the back of the earth
And search within my longings the intimate intrigue
Bewilder me in the flight of my fantasy bird
And leave a water rose hid in my fantasies.
Great Loíza River! My water springs, my river
Since the maternal petal ascended to the world
My pallid aspirations from the rough hills descended
With you to find new furrows;
My childhood as a whole, a poem in the river
A river in the poem of my very first dreams.

While the ACTRESS builds the image of her mother, the DANCER, who is now the mother, appears by the river, washing in its waters a sheet, which is also a shroud, a sail that provides visions of a voyage, and a flag that invites her to join her in the grave. At the end, the mother (DANCER) flees quickly with the sheet behind her.

ACTRESS
Almost human, the nightly cries have left[4]
She raised me in one spurt with her hand of stars
Her first caress, it was your laugh extended
Throughout my dawn, Oh, my river, dismayed with loss!

My dolls were made from your purple reeds,
My traveling hair strands, from your restless waves.
She did not want to see me if not tossing on gold
From your waters opened, and from their yellow kiss.

In your fountains, at the thirst of the lilies
From my chaste surrenders, live fireflies were birthed.
She did not braid the sprigs of my dreams
For a harmony other than my poetry wish.

Her sobs in your lips were a bird's breeze
Fatally divining my fate on your path.

She instructed you in my love, and was
White on your warm back, our first rendezvous.

---

[4] "Mi madre y el río."

Almost human, the cries penetrate my flesh.
She has left, Oh, my river, dismayed with loss!
She has left my hands like a missing rose
And left in my soul all her being in essence...
Oh, my river! Oh, my river! Because of her love I stopped
On long and agile mornings to search for you in the fog
Because of her love I went searching for you in the purest faces
'til I loved you in the man that erected my conscience.

I know that she wishes to embrace me in your arms:
She told me so one night, assaulted by stars.
Her intangible tenderness infiltrated my figure,
And, oh, my river! It is time to embellish her path.

Oh, the human cries! How they open my blood!
Oh, my river, free her earthly anchor!
And don't tell her I still am at a halt on the floor.
Let her quest for me amid stars, or in the jungles' voice.

When her mother (DANCER) disappears, the ACTRESS sees, at a distance, the figure of (HE) a worker (sugar cane cutter, or farmer), who is later joined by his wife (DANCER). The ACTRESS ends by saying, "We must chase darkness out of our land!" The two workers (HE and DANCER) hear her and interrupt their work to look at the ACTRESS from the distance. They are thinking about her command. Light slowly dims on DANCERS, who are now standing alert.

ACTRESS
That true path abandoned![5]
That girl who goes around barefoot knocking down butterflies!
That bitter morning, washing its face in the brook!

Countryside...
Farmer girl, scatterbrained, like the innocence filling your eyelids...
Taciturn seed that does not want spring in a land sleepless with questions...
Colt that saddles up tame a horizon armed with countryside cries...

Tradition has gone up in flames in the countryside!
Hope has gone up in flames in the countryside!
Man has gone up in flames in the countryside!

---

5 "Campo."

The white soil has luminous footsteps.
The black soil has arms of faith.
The red soil has lungs of wind.

There is much upright green leaving the hills to join the great fire
The reprisal of the furrows,
The burial of the sugar harvest.

Ripe!
The earth will sow its harvest of freed men!
We must chase darkness out of our land!

SCENE 2.

*ACTRESS alone, suspended in an undefined space. She recalls how HE came into her
life. As she shares her feelings with the audience, who is her sister or her other self, HE
approaches her from the back in slow, firm, sensual movements. He covers her eyes in a
childish gesture. She doesn't have to look back to know that it is HE. She turns around
and sees him. HE, at the end of the poem, takes the place of the ACTRESS.*

ACTRESS
With eyes closed, wide with intimate voices,[6]
I halt in the century of my sleeping sorrows.
I study it while it sleeps...
It sleeps its sad night
Uprooted from the ground whence my life begins.
The tame race of my soul no longer disturbs
Nor it goes to my face disguised in the pain of my pupils.

Enclosed in its shape,
It no longer shows the delicate contour of its fingers
Knocking down my joys,
Nor has it off tune rhythms
Within the perfect harmony of my erected song.

No longer splits my time...
It sleeps its sad night
Ever since you anchored yourself on the light of my rhymes.

I remember the hours would roll without image

---

[6] "Poema de mi pena dorminda."

Upon my raw sorrows,
Whenever your shadow ran across other peculiar shadows
In ownership of laughter.
My feelings awaited...
But I had moments of suicidal madness:
You were taking so long!
And the music conveyed by your echo was ample!

I remember you came basic in instincts.
You were also imbibing the centuries' wide sorrows;
But you were also stronger and in a splendid effort,
Exiled all your anguish and put all mine to sleep!

DANCERS explore each other, make love. At the end of the encounter, HE is exhausted, but DANCER is too excited to sleep. DANCER puts HE to sleep and watches over him, talking to herself, wishing the moment never ends. We hear the recorded voice of AC-TRESS again. This time, the recorded text has a background of electronic music.

Voice of ACTRESS (*recorded*)
On the roofs of my soul the doves are puzzled[7]
When your life ascends.

Air...
Air remains still.

There are a thousand bird mouths handling these songs
Above my budding meadow,
And the rebelling tremor of chaste butterflies
Breaks veils on its effort to see me.

My heart has heard a rumour
Of a misplaced wave,
And it has turned to the cosmos
In a silent quest...

How will they silence me
When all the echoes of the universe
Become symphonies on my forehead?

Loved one,

---

7 "Canción para dormirte."

Sleep, sleep...

The ACTRESS takes the place of the DANCER (by his side). HE is sleeping. ACTRESS talks to him and to herself.

ACTRESS
I am the night in wake in love...[8]

Surprisingly, birds do no follow me by the hundreds
Pecking songs over my white shadow.
Is it that they are enclosing, within sleepless clouds,
The immense lucidity where my soul moves forward?

Surprisingly, I am not being carried away by pale daisies
Through the lovely route my wings have taken.
Is it that they are crying over their saddest sister,
Who in silence has left at the break of dawn?

Surprisingly, the slightest of those soft breezes that put me to sleep
As a child is not dressing me up as a bride.
Is it that amid the trees it shows my loved one
The innocent furrows I walked upon, chaste?

Surprisingly, the dew is not throwing its emotions at me
As drops that reflect the beaming morning.
Is it that on the anguished furrows of the past
With generous waters it bathes my disappointments?

I am the night in wake in love...

Upon me songs and petal bunches drape,
And so do many white dreams and winged emotions.

Surprisingly, man does not understand me, confused
By the simple hand that gathered up my soul.
Is it that at night it looses its petals so slowly?
It may not understand emotions so distilled.
Do not remember me! Feel me![9]
There is only a song between your love and my soul.
Both my eyes navigate

---

8 "Amanecida."

The same endless blue where you dance.

Your rainbow of dreams has in me
Always an open meadow between the hills.
Once my sobs got lost
And I did find them, sheltered, in your tears.

Do not remember me! Feel me!
A nightingale has in its throat both you and me.

The rivers I brought with from my cliffs,
Flow into only just your beach.

There is bewilderment of flights throughout the air...
The wind carries us on its espadrilles!

Do not remember me! Feel me!
The less you think of me, the more you love me will.

SCENE 3.

ACTRESS retreats to her own space, away from him, to meditate about what she is feeling and about the impossibility of expressing it in words.

ACTRESS
Deep with you, I drown my heart in voices,[10]
While you sleep a dream of words...
Loved one! The night moves so full of stars!

The night's rose swings between the streets.
The echoes of swallows allay over the cloud.
The shadow dances its pain away across the docks.
The sea confronts the wind in its wild perfume.
And every now and then, ideals quake and blossom...

Through her poetry, she takes him on a space voyage, and creates a cosmic landscape which contrasts with her description of New York: slides of scenes of New York, or of hand, fragmented structures provide the mesh of light and darkness under which she

---

9 "Canción hacia adentro."

10 "Sueño de las palabras."

moves. The recorded voice is in counterpoint with her real voice.

ACTRESS

I've walked quite a bit around the city, and I've gotten lost a couple of times... Means of transportation here are very complicated. Imagine, nine million inhabitants just within the city radius. Most of them walk –here family life is uncommon– pushing each other on buses, stores, cafés, etc. All that people require streetcars, subways, and elevated trains, in such a way that they change direction in every corner and one must be an expert in its web.

Our lives have joined in space[11]
Absconding from themselves!
So light we feel
That the conductor of the wind delays its exit.
See upon us the memory of a dream,
And further yet a lily's feeble breath;
See how the gazes of the air slip away
Seeking the ultimate scent of an empty rose.

Two days after my arrival, full of self-confidence, I tried to move around on a double-decker bus, and unknowingly ended up in Long Island, a certainly distant part of the city, separated from it by an enormous bridge. Of course, one must use the head in these instances. I didn't get off the bus, assuming it would return to its point of departure. And so it did, although after taking a three-hour detour... But I didn't learn my lesson. Two days after that I got lost on the subway. I walked several streets under the ground, on the great underground avenues of New York, until I found my train. That is how you learn, and I am not afraid of going anywhere by myself.

From here I can see the sea with waves swimming into shore,[12]
And one can hear the face of a child who plays trying to reach his image...

Even the poem rolls now without words from my voice to your soul...
And to think that down there the form awaits us!

ACTRESS in in front of a white barren wall. She feels completely alone, although she knows that her lover is next to her. Se cannot define her anguish. It is something that has been with her long before meeting her lover. New York City starts to change for her: it is a cold, mechanical environment in which she feels alienated.

---

[11] "Principio de un poema sin palabras."

[12] "Principio de un poema sin palabras," continues.

ACTRESS
Nothing disturbs my being yet I am grieving.[13]
Something unhurried in shadows hits me,
Despite that almost behind this anguish,
I have had stars in my hands.

It must be the caress from the useless,
The endless sadness of being a poet,
Of singing and singing, without it breaking
The unsurpassed tragedy of existence.

To be and to not want to be... is the aphorism,
The battle that wears out all wait,
To find oneself, the soul already dying,
A wretched body where strength still remains.

Forgive me, oh love, if I don't name you!
Out of your song I am a dried up wing
Death and I sleep together...
Only singing to you awakes me.

"I am almost disconcerted in this country. Much more than now, during my first days
here. There were moments in which I wanted to go anywhere more serene and hospitable than here... It is not so much the terrible reality—a cold that freezes your bones,
and the feeling of routine and machinery—but the gigantic wave of efforts and obstacles
that I brought with me in my head from that land of mine, so hard of justice..."
                                                                                    New York. January 25, 1940.

"At the moment, everything in New York is covered by a thick fog, which gives the
impression of being part of a legend, or of a silenced world. I had never felt the city so
quiet, perhaps because the first months I spent here, if not the environment, my spirit, was always screaming because of some circumstances in my life, and how they had
ended; and yet today they only caress my existence. Today there is only one caress
that moves me: the realization of my most intimate dreams... Love's hand is with me
at all times, and I tell you, reality far surpasses the ideals we forge. I am completely
changed. My soul has found again its stream of endless calmness and fondness, and
time no longer comes before me to mercilessly separate me from the bosom whose
love surrounds my existence."
                                                                                    New York. April, 1940.

---

[13] "Canción amarga."

"You say there is something going on with me that runs deeper than what the eye meets on my words. But it is true that there is nothing abnormal going on. It is the environment that surrounds me, so balanced, that paradoxically throws my existence a bit off balance. It is this new lifestyle to which, at least on the outside, I must conform to, what primarily overwhelms and saddens me. You know about the rest. It is this I live, split in two, between essence and form, between the ruthless blow of circumstances, and the warm and soft echo of love calling me. It's the same sadness I suffered in Puerto Rico, only more defined, because here, the hope of a more complete happiness has been hurt, while there it was still fresh and expecting. But it will pass. In the meantime, I must be strong."

New York. March 1st, 1940.

DANCERS farewell. Both words and music are recorded.

ACTRESS

It's so bad to dream! Right? To then see our dreams torn to pieces... Mine have been true gusts of wind, and I always fall, dragged by my own wings, to end up tangled up in the most obstinate reality. He's leaving for Cuba next week, and he's leaving without me. I will leave later on. I thought our farewell in San Juan would be the last, and now you see it's happening again. Like this, the future will be all farewells and meetings, but never an uninterrupted reality full of caresses... I will always be his shadow in any social context, even if I know, in private, I still am his cradle, his backbone, as he is of my soul. Let's hope... I think I will die hoping.

SCENE 4.

Two nurses (DANCERS) appear. They are pushing a hospital bed covered with the sheet that the mother (Dancer) had washed in the river. ACTRESS has a nervous breakdown. They offer her a white flower and leave her. She discovers the flower is a symbol of her death and discards it. The DANCERS push the bed with the ACTRESS on it. She is aboard the boat that will take her to Cuba, where her lover awaits. Slow blackout.

ACTRESS

"You cannot fathom what I went through in New York. Those months almost destroyed my existence forever. My life never had cruel circumstances take over in such a way. Specially, the month and a half I spent without him. It almost drove me straight to madness. They had to care for me on the bus on my way to Florida. I almost had to stay at a clinic in Miami. I didn't want to tell you this as to not make you suffer. But I am telling you now that all risk of insanity has passed, so that you see that there are ills worse than economic need... But we must not despair. I am already in condition to fight, in a hospitable and humane environment. This way I will be able to help you as I would like, with all my spiritual strength."

Havana. July 9, 1940.

"For the first time, I have set foot on free land in Indo-Hispanic America! It's something great. I invoked Martí, and remembered all the Puerto Rican blood spilled in Cuba for the Independence cause. The Cuban flag, rising on every horizon, left in me the greatest feeling of sadness. It is so similar to its sister, ours, which undulates only in the few hearts that have known to keep it safe from the wind gusts that have stripped the majority of our people of its sense of shame. Never forget that in order to have real social justice in our land, call it communism or else, we must first have the flag that defines us as Hispanic Americans undulate freely and on its own."

Havana. June 27, 1940.

"I am delighted to be in this land. The readjustment of the world is near and it is interesting to be with a strong people, where efforts are not wasted. We'll see. Look how advanced it is all here that the candidate for mayor in Havana is none other than the great Hispanic American writer and thinker Juan Marinello. The great poet Nicolás Guillén is also running for mayor of Camagüey. Similarly, there are many smart and apt young people showing up to take control of civic matters. Even if they are not triumphant now, history will see that their effort comes to fruition. You will see how this will all end up, with the redemption of man: first will be justice, then freedom, until they merge in a tight embrace."

Trinidad. July 2, 1940.

Cuba, with its activity and beauty, makes her think of her homeland. ACTRESS has a vision of her countryside. She sees the trees of her land growing guided by sunlight, as an offering of the earth, as a symbol of combat and affirmation. The DANCERS embody the trees while the ACTRESS, now a young girl, plays among them with enthusiasm.

ACTRESS
They were rose apple and cherry.[14]
My trees!
They were much like me.
It was crazy to see me above the wind!
My eyes were a dream whenever they climbed up a cherry tree!
Childhood, like a child, has gone out to play with my affection.
What this child wants is not a story about wrath.
My childhood seeks childhood!
I remember the evening I cried over a sleepy plant
Because it wouldn't wake up.

---

[14] "Campo."

One day I stayed to contemplate, in madness, the horizon
And so the sun handed me tears.
My most intimate gift by the brook
Was to pinch my hands with pallid lemon tree branches
To then spill myself into the waters.

It seems the guava trees heard me at birth,
So did the dark slabs,
Because every so often they would mimic my cry,
Specially at night, when every hill
Would come down to the water.

And my trees!
Voluntary guardians of my childhood,
Flags without a country,
Shotguns of time directed only by earth!

My trees!
They will know how to care for you, farmer!
They will know how to grow from your tears!
They will know how to burn,
They will know how to strengthen you for the great conquest.

I am a grown child piling up the wreckage
Of a stolen innocence,
A child, bloody, hoisting its cry
Together with all the rags on my hills,
A village where childhood does not want to desist.

"I would not want to go to Puerto Rico for many reasons of a moral kind that you well know. I don't want to meet with certain people whom I've cut off from my existence, thanks to distance."

Havana. July 9, 1940.

HE approaches her silently, as in his first entrance, to offer her a ring.

ACTRESS
"He loves me more passionately every day, and every day he wants to shut me off from the world even more. He doesn't want me to wear nail polish if it's not a natural color, nor to wear make up around the house. And to top it all off, all of a sudden, he

has gifted me a wedding ring, which, by the way, makes me very happy. I will take my picture in a way that you can see the ring on my hand."

Santiago. January 13, 1941.

The DANCER is a bourgeois lady, seated in a gathering of ladies, talking about the inefficiency of their servants. DANCER duplicates some of the mannerisms that the ACTRESS accentuates as she talks about the ridiculous situation.

ACTRESS
"I lead a life most puritan than the most puritan of female mummies. I spend the day sewing, listening to the radio, and talking to the ladies in the guesthouse; by night, I rigidly sit in a formal meeting, commenting on the inaptitude of the maids, in keeping with my position as "wife." Whenever he meets, at any unexpected moment, on the street, with a family friend, he introduces me as his friend. (*She pauses, wanting to justify this as to not have to confront reality.*) He loves me in his own way, but thinks first and foremost about his mother, who's told him she would commit suicide if he married me. One day, he proposed we marry in secret. You can imagine all the things I said to him. Imagine that! I told him I could be his wife before men, regardless of relations. Otherwise, he could keep his charity, which I do not need.

July 14, 1941.

Across from her, she discovers her own distorted, superficial image. The DANCER is now the mirror image of the ACTRESS. There is a violent confrontation between the simple, free, poet (ACTRESS) and the frivolous, manipulated, artificial woman (DANCER). At the beginning, the DANCER ignores the confrontation: for a moment, she tries to confront her, but finally flees intimidated by the poet's force.

ACTRESS
People already rumor that I am your enemy[15]
Because they say in verse I give the world your self.
They lie, Julia de Burgos. They lie, Julia de Burgos.
The voice that rises in my verses is not yours: it's my voice;
Because you are the garments while the essence is I;
And the deepest void lies between the two.

You are the coldest doll made by society's lies,
And I the strongest glimmer of truth for humankind.

You, sweet courteous hypocrisies; not I.
In every single poem my heart I leave exposed.

---

15 "A Julia de Burgos."

You are just like your world, selfish; not I.
Who bets it all on being who I am.

You are just the grave missus, the lady; not I.
I am life, strength, woman.

You belong to your husband, your master; not I.
I am no one's, or everyone's, because to everyone, to everyone,
In my pure feelings and thoughts, I bequeath myself.

You curl your hair, wear make up; not I.
The wind curls up my hair, the sun colors my face.
You don't govern yourself; they all govern you:
You're governed by husband, your parents, family,
The tailor, the theatre, the casino, and the priest,
The car, the jewels, the banquet, the champagne,
Heaven and hell, and what people might say.

Not I. I am governed by solely my heart,
Solely my thoughts; who governs me is I.

You, aristocratic flower; I, the flower of the people.
You, within you, have everything, and owe it to everyone,
While I, my nothing, is to no one owed.

You, hammered to static ancestral divisions,
And I, a one in the figure of social divide,
We are a duel to the death, fatally approaching.

When the unruly crowds run
Leaving behind the ashes of injustices burned,
And when with the torch of the seven virtues
The crowds run after the seven sins,
Against you and against everything unjust and inhumane,
I will run amidst them with the torch on my hand.

Alone, she confronts the audience with these words:

ACTRESS
I wanted to be like men wanted me to be:[16]

An attempt of life,
A game of hide and seek with my being.
But I was made of presents,
And my feet, flat over the promising land
Could not bear to walk back,
And they kept moving forward, forward,
Outwitting the ashes in order to reach the kiss
Of the new paths.

With each step forward into the route ahead
My back was torn apart by the desperate wingbeat
Of old trunks.
But the branch had been detached forever
And with each new lash my gaze
Moved away more and more and more from the distant
Learned horizons;
And my face took on the expression that came to it from the inside,
The defined expression that showed a feeling
Of intimate liberation;
A feeling that emerged
From the balance sustained between my life
And the truth told by the kiss of the new paths.

Once my path in the present was defined,
I felt myself a sprout of all the soils on earth,
Of all the soils without a history,
Of all the soils without a future,
Of the soil forever soil without a border
Of all men and all ages.

And I was all in me just like life was within me...

I wanted to be like men wanted me to be:
An attempt of life,
A game of hide and seek with my being.
But I was made of presents;
When the heralds were already announcing me
In the sumptuous procession of old trunks,
My wish to follow men was warped,

---

16 "Yo fui mi misma ruta."

And the homage was left waiting for me.

"The obstacles removed, the will has not responded accordingly, and there are no more alternatives left. We've talked about everything. I've received huge blows I never expected. My only refuge now is my studies. I have clung to them with true frenzy. I've had various partial exams these days, all approved with distinctions. I am satisfied with myself, and confident, more than ever."

Havana. April 22, 1942.

"Sometimes, in order to save something beautiful, one must destroy it, so that it doesn't wither and become corrupted in our own miserable hands. I can tell you nothing else. Please, understand me. When I think about how I even abandoned you in the greatest of tragedies to follow him into exile, my heart wants to burst. (*She pauses, and reflects, trying to find a positive angle.*) What is urgent is trying to find a new beginning in life. I will try to drown in the painful instant of the world as to not feel this loneliness so deep in my bones. I must make a trip... But I will not abandon my studies. Against all adversity, I will try to triumph at least in something, see the results of my own efforts. That will be my answer to the latest blows."

June 8, 1942.

No one.[17]
I was on my own.
No one.
Coloring daybreaks with my one color of loneliness.
No one.

Repeating myself in all desperations.
Quieting in my insides the cry to seek you.
Adding up ideals in each broken thruth.
Hurting the sprigs with my mourning to erect you.

Oh, vanished one!
How I grafted my soul on the blue to find you!
And like that, a madwoman looking up,
Seething my eyes in the reddest light to fulfill you,
How I followed the flight of my most avid emotion
Through the hospitable crepuscular gold!

Until there was a morning...

---

[17] "Poema detenido en un amanecer."

A night...
An evening...
I was left like a huddled up dove
And I found my eyes by your blood.

Godly sunrises
Marvellously woke my valleys.

Landslides!
Riverbeds!
Swallows! Stars!
Hard and agile daybreaks!

All within you:
Savage sun!

And me?
–A simple truth to love you...

"He arrived at noon on Friday from the Cuban countryside with the sweet gift of a ticket for the 4pm flight. It was all horrible, including arriving at the station, without anyone there waiting for me. Having had no sleep in 48 hours, I had to get out there and find a room to rent, and eat, with a meager five dollars. (*Pauses to analyze his behavior.*) He found a chance to wash his hands like Pilate. (*Pauses.*) Sleepy and hungry, I went out there to try to find old friends, but they're all gone..."

Man River, but a man with the purity of a river,[18]
Because you give your blue soul as you give your blue kiss.
Very sir, my river. Man River. The only man
Who has kissed my soul as he kisses my body.

Scene 5.
"He generously let time run its course. (*Pauses.*) That which was so enormous is now dead. Pain has turned into indignation, not at him, but at man itself. For me, he does not exists, only humanity. And how poor it is! I wrote him a heartbreaking farewell that could not be delayed. After twenty days of freedom, I am back to my old self. And here I am, crying, not because of pain, but out of disappointment."

New York. July 12, 1942.

---

[18] From "Río Grande de Loíza."

Since life is nothing in your school of thought,[19]
Let's toast for the certain not being of our bodies.

Let's toast for the nothingness of your sensual lips
Which are sensual zeroes in your blue kisses;
Like everything blue, chimeric falsehood
From the white oceans, and the white skies.

Let's toast for the nothingness of the material claim
That sinks and rises in your carnal desire;
Like all that is flesh, lightning, spark,
In the endless lying truth of the Universe.

Let's toast for the nothingness, no good of your soul,
That rides its falsehood on an unstoppable colt;
Like all that is nothing, good nothing not even
Suddenly peeks in a brief glint.
Let's toast for ourselves, for them, and no one;
For the ever nothingness of our never bodies.
For everyone, at least; for so many and so nothing;
For all those hollow shadows of the living who are dead.

If we come from not being, and to not being we march,
Nothing between nothing and nothing, zero between zero and zero,
And if between nothing and nothing, nothing cannot exist,
Let's toast for the beautiful not being of our bodies.

For the day of shadows that will come, my love[20]
Like a cliff pouring over a spring,
For the day of horrors and handkerchiefs to the wind
Let's start singing since life is at the brink.

Let's sing, yes, let's sing, we have only a minute
One only, awaiting for our world to cross:
The tragic minute that's been wandering around us for a while now
With its offer of tears and restless mornings.

They will take you! The echoes in the wind tell me,

---

[19] "Nada."

[20] "Te llevarán."

The sea lips cry they will. They will take you!
You will leave, and my eyes, which nurtured you so,
Will go down quietly to nurture the sea.

Loved one, my executioner has already measured my step,
The color of my footstep they know, and my grave goods:
Modesty puts eternal weddings to sleep together with the form;
The way to the soul is too long a walk.

They will take you! To an eternity of tears.
Let's start singing since life is at the brink.
For the day of horrors and handkerchiefs to the wind
The song of death will come to us from the sea.

Sea of mine,[21]
Deep sea who starts within me,
Sea alone and underground
From my land of tight swords.

Sea of mine,
Nameless sea,
Turbid gorge in my devastated song,
Broken and disconcerted overseas silence,
Desperate blue,
Seabed,
Seagrave...

Blue,
Livid blue,
For my bloodied buds,
For the absence of my smile,
For the voice that conceals my death behind poems...
Sea of mine,
Seabed,
Nameless sea,
Sea unexpected,
Sea in the foam of a dream,
Sea in loneliness, wedding the dusk,
Sea breeze baring naked my ultimate commotion,
Sea you,

---

[21] "Letanía del mar."

Sea universe...

I have had to give, multiply myself,[22]
Tear myself into complex orbits...
Here in private, with myself,
What simplicity shatters my conscience!

To save the world from my spirit,
I've had to arm my peaceful hands,
How I long for peace, the noiseless time,
When nothing disturbs my own existence!

All sound has died in my pupils
My eyes are not worried with the stars,
Paths are free from my course,
And even the name of the sea deafens me.

And yet they ask me for songs in stead of words,
They can't conceive of my heartbeat without poems,
In my walk they seek quavering stars,
As if I didn't walk upon this land!

Oh, slowness of the sea! Oh, the brief footstep
With which death approaches my dead wing!
How would I do to save the time for you?
Of the world, what's left for me? What's left for me...?

"I want to go to Puerto Rico as soon as possible to join in the efforts to completely free our country. I feel a bit guilty about so much and such prolonged a distance, but you know it has had to be this way for various reasons."

Washington. January 22, 1945.

"Prepare your trip calmly, for when the Puerto Rican flowers are open, waiting for my arrival, and when the beaches wear their most beautiful blue to welcome my life, whole and healthy like before. I'd like to spend a couple of days by the sea, basking under the sun, like in the days of our youth, and to be able to see my river again, with the same longing and tranquil eyes I had when I was its girlfriend."

April 7, 1953.

---

22 "Oh, lentitud del mar."

Great Loíza River... Great river. Great cry.[23]
The greatest among all of our islander cries
If it weren't greatest the one springing from me
Through the eyes of my soul for my enslaved people.

I, fatalist,[24]
Looking at life come by and move away
From my fellow men.

I, inside my self,
Always waiting for something
That my mind cannot guess right.

I, multiple,
Like in a contradiction,
Tied to a feeling without a shore
That ties me and unties me,
Alternately,
To the world.

I, universal,
Imbibing life
In each exorbitant star,
In each sterile cry,
In each feeling without a shore.

And all, what for?
–In order to continue being myself.

Voice of ACTRESS (*recorded*)
1952. I've been in hospital for five years; a liver condition.
December 29, 1952. My vocal chords are ill and are operated on.

ACTRESS
"I crave for freedom. If I die, I don't want this tragic country to swallow my bones.
They need the warmth of Borinquen, so that at least they strengthen the worms over
there, and not those over here."

Goldwater Memorial Hospital, Ward D-12

---

[23] From "Río Grande de Loíza."

[24] "Momentos."

What are they waiting for? Are they not calling me?[25]
Have they forsaken me amongst the leaves,
My most simple comrades,
All the deceased of the earth?

Why won't they ring their bells?
I am in readiness waiting for the leap.
Perhaps they'd like the corpses
Of yet more dead dreams of innocence?

Perhaps they'd like more wreckage
From yet more drizzled springs,
Yet more dry eyes in the clouds,
Yet more hurting faces in the storms?

Would they like the wind's coffin
Huddled up amongst my hair?
Do they want the stream's yearnings,
Dead in my poet's mind?

Would they like the sun taken apart,
Already exhausted in my vessels?
Would they like the shadow of my shadow,
To be where there are no stars left?
I can't almost bear the world
That's lashing my conscience with its all.

Call my number! I don't want
Even love to disengage from me...
(Together with me is a dream that follows me
Just like my footsteps to my footprints.)

Call my number, because otherwise
I will die past my demise!

---

[25] "Dadme mi número."

SCENE 6.

The nurses (DANCERS) come to sedate her. They put her in bed, examine her, give her shots and tranquilizers, and another white flower, which, exhausted, she accepts this time.

ACTRESS
My soul?[26]
A broken harmony
That goes around bouncing its madness
Off the cushion of time.

How they want it to lean back,
To adapt,
To recompose,
Mortals that have long been dead!

Determination plummeting into achievement.
Loud-mouthed!

"Things have gotten worse again at this hospital. There's a spiritual chaos above all. I just spoke to the doctors and they say the liver test results came back very good, and that I am physically fit to be discharged, but I still need to become mentally balanced, so they will have to leave me here for longer."

The madness in my soul[27]
Cannot lean back,
It lives in the uneasiness,
The commotion,
The instability,
Of dynamic things,
In the silence
Of the free thinker, who lives by himself,
In quiet exile.

"I think what they want is for me to finally go mad so that they can commit me to some institution. It's true I have personal issues, but they worsen in such servitude and uncertainty. I spend whole days in extreme nervousness. I am not given any medication, just food and a bed."

---

[26] "Mi alma."

[27] "Mi alma," continues.

A strong broken harmony
The one in my soul;
Broken from birth;
Sows today, more than ever,
Its innate rebelliousness
In stilts of strategic leaps.

"They say I'm O.K., but when I am most serene they put me up on a stretcher and exhibit me to every medical student in the city. Yesterday, I became infuriated with so much annoyance, and I didn't touch my food. They punished me in the afternoon by putting me in bed. They threatened with kicking me out of the hospital, despite the fact that I don't have anywhere else to go. Today, I am calmer but I don't know what they will decide."

May 15, 1953.

A parachute is slowly lifted by the center to create a vertical, hollow structure: cave? inner space? death?

ACTRESS
To die with myself, abandoned and alone[28]
On the most solid rock of a deserted island
In this instant, the greatest yearning for carnations
And in this view, a tragic horizon made of stones.

My eyes all filled with tombs for the celestial bodies,
And my passion, laid down, spent, dispersed.
My fingers like children, watching clouds disappear
And my reason inhabited by bed sheets so immense.

My pallid affection returning to silence,
–Even love, brother melted in my path!–
My name untwisting, yellow on the branches,
And my hands convulsing to give me to the grass.
To incorporate myself on the last, essential minute,
To offer myself to the fields with the purity of a star
To fold then the leaf of my simple flesh,
And to go down without a smile, nor witness to the inertia.
Let no one profane my death with sobs,
Nor cover me forever with innocent soil;
In the freest moment may they leave me freely
Make use of the only liberty in the planet.

---

[28] "Poema para mi muerte."

Voice of ACTRESS (*recorded*)
With such ferocious happiness my bones will start[29]
To search for little windows through the brown flesh
And I, giving myself, giving myself, fierce and freely
Under the open sky and alone breaking my chains!

Who will be able to stop me with futile illusions
When my soul begins to accomplish its task,
Making my dreams a fertile mess
For the fragile worm that will knock on my door?

Smaller each time my smallness exhausted,
Greater each instant and simpler my bequeath,
My bosom may roll to begin a cocoon,
Perhaps my lips will nourish the madonnas.

What name will I have when the only thing left
Is to remember me, on the rock of a deserted island?
A carnation lodged between the wind and my shadow,
The son of mine and of death, will call me poet.

ACTRESS
"I write to you from the island's bridge, where I've escaped to from all the doctors for a few minutes. It's all enclosed on my floor. Temperature is set at 75. I need fresh air. I'm only wearing a hospital gown. I discovered a post from which I could send you this brief letter before the nurses come to take me back to bed. I feel pretty strong. The social worker has given me two little dresses and some shoes that will be good for my release. I have an old gown, but I wash it every day. If you can, send me a couple of bucks to buy toothpaste, soap, talcum powder, and a pair of slippers. I look forward to the guava paste..."

June, 1953.

DANCER is on the stoop of a building: tries to get up to continue walking. Her impulse fails. She falls.

Voice of ACTRESS (*recorded*)
It has to be from here,[30]
Forgotten but unshaken
Among comrades of silence

---

[29] "Poema para mi muerte," continues.

Deep into Welfare Island
My farewell to the world.

Voice of HE *(recorded), with the affectation of a news reporter*
It is August 8, 1953. Reporting for *El Mundo*. Julia de Burgos was found unconscious
at 105th street off 5th Avenue. She passed away almost immediately upon transfer
to Harlem Hospital. The body, dispossessed of any sort of identification, was taken
to the city morgue. Police attempts to identify the body failed. A photograph of the
body was key in solving the mystery. A month had passed by the time all details about
the painful incident had been completely recreated. The death certificate indicates
lobular pneumonia as the cause of death. There were no documents, bags, or identification on the body.

Slow blackout.

EPILOGUE.
*ACTRESS inside tent created by the parachute. DANCER slowly rises as the poet reaf-
firms herself in her poetry. Both parts, woman and poet, are reunited with a sense of
self-assurance. They are mirror images at the end. They hold still for a long moment,
after which the music breaks in as the lights fade.*

ACTRESS and DANCER *in unison*
In the riverbank of death,[31]
There is something,
Some voice,
Some sail about to leave,
Some empty grave
Which captivates my soul.

In the riverbank of death,
So close!, in the riverbank
(which is like contemplating myself arriving at a mirror)
even the song and the color of my name
can recognize me.

Am I the itinerant bridge between slumber and demise?
Present!

---

[30] From "Farewell to Welfare Island."

[31] "Entre mi voz y el tiempo."

From where in the world are they calling, from which front?
I am in the open sea...

Amidst time...
Who will prevail?
Present!
Am I alive?
Am I dead?
Present! Here! Present!

Slow blackout.

END OF PLAY

SANTACLOS IN BORINKEN (1979)

CHARACTERS
SANTACLOS
RUDOLPH
GASPAR, has brown hair and beard, wears a green cloak and a crown
MELCHIOR, has long, white hair, wears a gold cloak and a crown
BALTHAZAR, is dark-skinned, has a black beard and wears a purple cloak, and a crown
ELVES
REINDEER

ACT 1

SETTING

Santa's workshop room at the Ice Palace in the North Pole. On the background, under a clear, deep blue sky, elves work atop an ice stage located underneath enormous and sparkling stalactites. On a nearby spot, young and energetic reindeer play boxing, run after each other, warm up and exercise. Either hanging from the ceiling or on a wall, there is a map of the Americas; Santaclos has drawn a red circle around the island of Borinken. Elves come in and out, extremely busy with their toy making. They've produced in excess: one can see brimming piles of gifts throughout the workshop. Amid the surplus, to work seems obsessive and disproportionate. There is a thick atmosphere filled with efficiency, movements are depersonalized and isolated to maximize production. There are different attitudes toward the situation in the group. Rudolph, the height of efficiency, supervises the elves and imparts discipline when the reindeer play rough with each other. No one makes fun of him. Santaclos comes in.

SANTACLOS
Rudolph, may I see you for a moment? This is urgent.

RUDOLPH
Yes, Sir.

SANTACLOS
I have good news for you.
(*To the ELVES*) I have good news for everybody. How would you like to take a trip to a tropical island?

ELVES chat among themselves without halting their work completely.

SANTACLOS
What do you think, Rudolph?

RUDOLPH
That would be a nice change, Sir.

SANTACLOS
Well, this Christmas we're going to a new island.

RUDOLPH
A new island?

SANTACLOS
Well, not exactly new. It's been there for centuries, but it's new for us. A new adventure. Our cute little helpers are working marvelously. We can produce toys for the whole world if we wanted to. New people, new sights to see. How's your Spanish Rudolph?

RUDOLPH makes a "so, so" hand gesture.

SANTACLOS
Enough to translate letters? That's all we need, really.

RUDOLPH
I can do it, Sir. I have a good dictionary. And there's still some time left to learn more.

SANTACLOS
Excellent. We must plan the trip. What do you suggest, Rudolph?

RUDOLPH
What is this "new" island, Sir?

SANTACLOS
It is called Borinken.

RUDOLPH looks in his maps and encyclopedias while SANTACLOS supervises the ELVES, who exaggerate their efficiency in his presence.

RUDOLPH
There is a problem, Sir. Someone already serves the island of Borinken.

SANTACLOS
And who is that?

RUDOLPH
The Three Wise Men. They visit every year on January 6. They've been visiting for four centuries.

SANTACLOS
Three against one. We'll see. We have to do something about that. What do you suggest, Rudolph?

RUDOLPH
Before you make any plans, I think it's best to have a talk with them... come to an agreement.

SANTACLOS
What kind of an agreement?

RUDOLPH
Well, we'll have to know what they're up to. I suggest we invite them to the Ice Palace. They must know a lot about the *Island of Enchantment*. They must know every kid by name. They have valuable information.

SANTACLOS
You're a smart cookie, Rudolph. I'll increase your hay ration one of these days.

RUDOLPH
Thank you, Sir.

SANTACLOS
Arrange the visit.
(*To the* ELVES) OK, fellows, keep it up. We must keep up the production, but first we must tidy up the Palace. We are having important guests. These foreign visitors must have a good impression about us. Straighten your suits. Brush your teeth. Polish your shoes. Comb your hair. Put everything in its place, and have a place for everything. Smile. Be polite.

ELVES start to frantically follow his instructions.

SANTACLOS
HO, HO, HO.

(Clears his throat. Sprays it with a small bottle. Tries again.) HO, HO, HO. That's better.

The doorbell rings.

RUDOLPH
I'll get it.

Before RUDOLPH makes it to the door the THREE WISE MEN appear upon a cloud and ceremoniously bow to SANTACLOS. Everyone is impressed by their appearance.

ALL
Wow!

RUDOLPH
What an entrance!

SANTACLOS
By your entrance I take it you're the Magi.

GASPAR *bows*
We are also called kings, or wise. We are priests, and astrologers, also experts in divining dreams. I am Gaspar, a scholar from India and King of Sheba.

MELCHIOR *bows*
I am Melchior, a scholar from Persia and King of Arabia. And a long time ago, we followed the Star of Bethlehem. It took us to baby King Jesus. Gaspar gave him frankincense, and I gifted him gold.

BALTHAZAR *bows*
And I brought Jesus myrrh. I am King Balthazar of Tarse. To celebrate that evening, every year, on the night of January 5th, we leave presents to children all around the world: Spain, the Philippines, Paraguay, Uruguay, Argentina, Mexico, Cuba, the Dominican Republic and, of course, Borinken. What's your story?

RUDOLPH
At your service.

SANTACLOS
I'm Santa Claus. Pleased to meet you. Please, sit down. Rudolph, bring three chairs for our guests. Three thrones, rather. That will be perfect for kings.

GASPAR

That will not be necessary, Mr. Claus. We're fine this way. We're a little tired from sitting on those humps.

SANTACLOS

Humps?

MELCHIOR

Yes, our camels' humps.

BALTHAZAR

Which reminds me... We left them out in the cold. They must be freezing. They're not used to this weather.

GASPAR

Yes, it's chilly up here, to say the least.

MELCHIOR

We come from the east, you see. We're not used to this weather.

SANTACLOS

Rudolph, see that their camels are comfortable.

RUDOLPH

Yes, Sir. (*Exits.*)

In the background, the ELVES watch while working.

SANTACLOS

(To the Magi) Please, make yourselves at home. Is it warm enough for you?

BALTHAZAR *shivering but courteously*

Yes, sure.

SANTACLOS

Let me show you my factory. This is the Season, you know. It gets very hectic around here. We receive a lot of mail from kids all over the world. And each year we try to go to new places to expand, and to invent new toys.

SANTACLOS shows the MAGI some of their new toys. They examine them.

SANTACLOS
What do you think, ah? Pretty clever, ah?

RUDOLPH *examining them*
Yes, they are nice.

SANTACLOS
These are my helpers. I'm sorry I can't introduce you to my reindeer; they're resting for the trip. Let me show you my sleigh. (*ELVES push the sleigh.*) We're improving on it. It has power steering, a stereo system, a refrigerator for sodas and sandwiches...

RUDOLPH *enters*
Is everything OK, Sir?

SANTACLOS
Yes, thank you, Rudolph. I'll take care of the gentlemen. You can go and exercise. You have to be in good shape for the trip.

RUDOLPH puts on tennis shoes and runs from one end of the room to the other while SANTACLOS talks to the KINGS.

BALTHAZAR
How can we help you?

SANTACLOS
What?

MELCHIOR
What can we do for you? You called us...

SANTACLOS
Oh, yes. It is about the *Island of Enchantment*. I am planning to visit there. I understand that you have been visiting the children of the island for three centuries. Do you have any suggestions, any warnings, any information on how things are there?

GASPAR
It is a beautiful island. It's warm; people are friendly.

MELCHIOR
They have a lot of fun in Christmas. They surprise people with *asaltos* and then sing *parrandas*.

SANTACLOS
That sounds good.

BALTHAZAR
But the children there are happy with the toys we bring them.

GASPAR
It is true that we still have to work on an equitable distribution.

MELCHIOR *to SANTACLOS*
But you'll probably have the same problem.

SANTACLOS
I understand that people there are starting to hear about me, and that they want me to come visit.

BALTHAZAR
And where did you get that information?

SANTACLOS
Well, there was a survey... My popularity is increasing, and I must not disappoint the children there. I don't want my reputation ruined.

MELCHIOR
And what do you want us to do?

SANTACLOS
I just wanted to have a friendly conversation with you, to ask you questions about the place, since you know it so well, so I can prepare for the trip and do the best possible job I can.

GASPAR
We cannot tell you anything. The best way to find out is to go the way we went for the first time, and learn from the children themselves. They know what they want. They can tell you about themselves and about their island.

SANTACLOS
Gee, since I have a communications problem, I thought maybe you...

MELCHIOR
It wasn't easy for us. When we arrived there for the first time there were native people called *taínos* that had never heard about us.

SANTACLOS

You know, I used to speak Russian, my native language, but I must admit I'm out of practice. I've changed somewhat. When I came to America I was different, I used to be very happy and funny. I laughed a lot. But lately... Can I tell you something? I've been loosing it. It is harder to laugh these days. You see, I have a lot of work to do. I can't be laughing and joking all the time. I must supervise my workers, I have to plan ahead, I have to increase production, keep up with the modern ways, invent new toys: space toys, electric toys, look-alike weapons. Kids love to play with death, you know?

BALTHAZAR

Mr. Santaclos, we are sorry we are unable to help you.

SANTACLOS

What about distribution? I am planning to go there on Christmas. The kids will be receiving my toys before you get there. Does that pose a problem to you? I don't want you to think that I am trying to drive you out of there. But I have the right to go if the children of the *Island of Enchantment* request that I go.

GASPAR

Good luck. We will be there planning our January 6 trip. We love the island. We go there before the 6th to plan and relax a little.

SANTACLOS

Where do you stay?

MELCHIOR

Different places. You'll have no trouble finding us.

GASPAR

Just like you didn't have any trouble communicating with us today.

SANTACLOS

That's amazing. How do you do it?

MELCHIOR

It's a long story as old as the centuries we came from.

GASPAR

Tell me something, what do you get out of this?

SANTACLOS
I don't know exactly. I like adventure.

BALTHAZAR
And mystery?

SANTACLOS
Yes, and the attention they give me during my Season. Many children think of me, write me letters. It makes me feel powerful. I can answer people's needs. I am on top of the situation. I am a doer, you know? I can't sit back and wait for others to do. I must get in there and cause changes...

GASPAR
Yes, it is nice to have people's attention.

SANTACLOS
Tell me, do you work as a team?

MELCHIOR
Yes, we've travelled together for a long, long time. We come from different places, but feel like brothers. We decide things together. We plan together. We work together. We learn from each other.

SANTACLOS
You'll probably have less to do if I start going to the *Island of Enchantment*. You'll be able to relax, take a break for a while. I'll take care of things for you.

GASPAR
No, thank you. There is a lot to be done there.

SANTACLOS
Do you resent my going there?

MELCHIOR
We will not stop you. Go and find out for yourself.

GASPAR
The children will decide what they want.

MELCHIOR
We must go now.

SANTACLOS
Would you like some tea and cookies?

BALTHAZAR
No, thanks. We have a lot of work to do.

SANTACLOS
I'll see you to the door.

They exit. RUDOLPH is running around the room. ELVES are still working. SANTA-CLOS returns visibly confused.

SANTACLOS
Interesting people... Rudolph!

RUDOLPH
Yes, Sir. How did it go?

SANTACLOS
Not so well.

RUDOLPH
Were you able to get some information?

SANTACLOS
No. They politely told me I have to go there and find out for myself.

RUDOLPH
Do you think they'll give you trouble?

SANTACLOS
Trouble? No, they seem to be very nice gentlemen. They'll just let me do what I want. I think they were impressed with our workshop. Well... we have to get ready. Bring the letters.

RUDOLPH *to the elves*
Bring the letters from the *Island of Enchantment*!

The ELVES can hardly drag the sacks. They leave them next to Rudolph and Santaclos.

RUDOLPH *takes one out and reads*
"Cheeky Santa..."

SANTACLOS
"Cheeky?" How's that?

RUDOLPH
No, no, sorry, got that wrong. *Cuerudo, querido...* Dear, it means dear.
"Dear Santa,
How are you? Hello to your helpers and reindeer, especially to Rudolph. (*RUDOLPH
smiles.*) Last year I asked the Three Kings to bring me a dump truck, a bicycle, a shotgun, a cowboy costume, a bazooka, a knife, a pair of skates, a superman costume, and
a pair of tennis shoes, and they only brought a toy car and some notebooks for school.
It seems the Three Kings are very serious and don't have time to get the toys I want.
My parents are very poor and can't buy me notebooks; that's why the Kings brought
those. My parents say the Kings are good people and bring useful things. Since you
are not so serious, could you bring everything else?"

SANTACLOS *with an ironic expression on his face*
Thank you! Is that the image they have of me? Not a serious guy, eh?

RUDOLPH
It's your laugh, Sir. They think you're always happy and don't have any problems.

SANTACLOS
I have news for them.

RUDOLPH
What do we do with this one?

SANTACLOS
Give him one of the toys. We have no room for everything he asks for.

The ELVES put a bazooka in the sack lying in the sleigh.

RUDOLPH
Here's the next one.
"Dear Santaclos,
Although the Three Kings have been very good to me, I write to you because I'd like
more toys. I won't dare ask more of them since that'd be abuse. You, on the other
hand, are rich and can bring me many toys. I'd like a dollhouse, and a doll that can

laugh, cry, dance, sing, run, cook, and that can take my place at school. I haven't seen such dolls around here but I know you have many kinds of toys and can build new ones as you like."

SANTACLOS
Who does she think I am?

RUDOLPH
They know you're efficient and very modern.

SANTACLOS
I can see this is not going to be a picnic.

RUDOLPH
What do we do with this one?

SANTACLOS
Just give her a regular doll. Give her one that cries and wets. That should be good enough.

RUDOLPH
Next one.
"Hello Chubby,
I heard that you are planning to come visit the *Island of Enchantment...*"

SANTACLOS
These kids have no respect. Everybody used to respect me. I used to bring toys and help little children. I remember how it was back home. Everybody loved me. Here, people are less formal. In Italy, true, I had some problems. They associated me with thieves, can you imagine? Do I look like the patron of thieves and criminals? Do you think these kids know anything about my past? No. They go for what they hear. That's why we have to go to the island, to show how serious and concerned with my work I am.

RUDOLPH
I think they call you 'chubby' out of friendliness.

SANTACLOS touches his belly
I don't like it.

RUDOLPH
You should jog with me every morning, Sir. It is very good.

SANTACLOS
Forget it, Rudolph. Go on with the letters.

RUDOLPH
"Dear Santa,
Why do you have a woman's name? Is it because of your long hair?"

SANTACLOS
What kind of nonsense is that?

RUDOLPH
Santa means female saint in Spanish, Sir.

SANTACLOS
Now they're gonna question my masculinity.

RUDOLPH
Should we answer explaining?

SANTACLOS
No. Go on with the letter. What does he want?

RUDOLPH
She. She wants... (*Reading and translating*) ...new shoes for her father. The ones he has are broken down and no good to take to work. A new dress for her mother, who works a lot and has no time for herself. "Don't tell her I wrote to you..."

SANTACLOS
And for herself?

RUDOLPH *reading and translating*
Nothing. She says she doesn't want to be pushy, that if she asks for too much you won't bring anything at all.

SANTACLOS
Nice, for a change. But we don't have shoes and dresses for adults. Just bring her a doll. She'll be happy.

RUDOLPH *picks out a new letter*
"Dear Santa,
I have been very good. I broke all of my last year's toys, but I'm sorry. I got tired of

them. I asked my parents to take me to Niagara Falls, where you live, but they are too busy now."

SANTACLOS
Niagara Falls? Where does he get his information?

RUDOLPH
They have three cars, a summerhouse, and a barbecue set. (*Reads*) "But I get bored since I have to stay by myself... They give me a lot of toys, but sometimes they send me away when they have parties. I am going to wait up for you. If I fall asleep, please wake me up. In the meantime, please, bring me a set of pistols, real ones, with bullets. They're just for protection. See you soon! P.S.: You must be wondering where I learned my English, right? I go to a Catholic private school. They teach everything in English, and they teach us about you. They say it is very important to learn English if you want to get a good job when you grow up. I don't like work, but I want to be rich when I grow up."

SANTACLOS
That little brat.

RUDOLPH
What shall we do?

SANTACLOS
What does he want to see me for?

RUDOLPH
It's hard to tell... What about the pistols?

SANTACLOS
Give them to him.

RUDOLPH
But he wants real ones.

SANTACLOS
Give him big ones. It should compensate for not being real.

RUDOLPH
Next one...

SANTACLOS
That's enough for now. I have a headache.

RUDOLPH
Are you worried, Sir?

SANTACLOS
Me, worried? No. If only I had more information.

RUDOLPH
About what?

SANTACLOS
About this *Island of Delights.*

RUDOLPH *clears throat and corrects him*
Of *Enchantment.*

SANTACLOS
Of *Enchantment.* What will we find there?

RUDOLPH *sings*

THE ISLAND OF ENCHANTMENT SONG

This is what we'll find
A tropical paradise
Exotic animals
Friendly locals
A never-ending spring
Fruits and flowers blooming

SANTACLOS feels relieved and signals the ELVES to join in the singing. They all sing The Island of Enchantment Song despite the fact that the ELVES are visibly tired. The ELVES collapse at the end of the song, while SANTACLOS then practices his laugh and RUDOLPH puts his dictionary in the sleigh.

The lights go out and we hear jingle bells and the sound of the wind in the darkness. We hear RUDOLPH and SANTA chatting softly in the background. Then we hear the sleigh brake, and a splash.

SANTACLOS
Oh, my god! What happened?

RUDOLPH
We're stuck, Sir.

END OF ACT 1

ACT 2

CHARACTERS
SANTACLOS
RUDOLPH
ELVES
REINDEER
POLICEMAN
MASKED MAN 1
MASKED MAN 2
(2) VOICES

SETTING
In the background, we see birds and butterflies, sunflowers and poppies, a bamboo forest and giant ferns. The full moon shines over the scenery; it has thin golden rays around it. There is also a mysterious blue light shining onto the scene. We can hear the sound of the bamboo shoots waving in the breeze. In the foreground, we see the sleigh, stuck in the mud. Rudolph's clothing is stained. Rain is pouring down. SANTACLOS is still unsettled by the accident. The other REINDEER have gotten loose and are exploring their surroundings.

SANTACLOS
Are you all right, Rudolph?

RUDOLPH groans a bit and takes his time

SANTACLOS
Rudolph!

RUDOLPH *gets up and inspects himself*
I think I broke a horn.

SANTACLOS *inspects RUDOLPH*
No, your horns are all right. I wonder where we are.

RUDOLPH *looks at the maps*
According to our maps, this must be Utuado. Sorry I lost control. Everything was going so well; then I started to get dizzy.

SANTACLOS
It must be the heat. It was a long trip. You're not used to this weather.

RUDOLPH
I hope the toys didn't break.

SANTACLOS
No, they're all right. Let's start to work.

SANTACLOS gets out of the sleigh, putting his foot in a puddle. He smiles as if to not make much of it.

SANTACLOS
Cheer up, Rudie.

A dog barks in the distance.

SANTACLOS
There must be a house around here. Let's make our first visit.

A car speeds by and splashes SANTACLOS, who tries to remain calm and in a good mood. He picks the sack of toys and puts it on his shoulder.

SANTACLOS
You take care of the sleigh. I'll do my job. (*Looking in his lists.*) Let's see, Utuado. (*Exits.*)

RUDOLPH inspects the damage on the sleigh, cleans himself a little, tries to find shelter from the rain, gets out an umbrella and looks at the maps. We hear dogs barking and trash cans falling down. SANTACLOS returns, looking confused.

RUDOLPH
What happened?

SANTACLOS
I couldn't find the chimney.

RUDOLPH
That's right. I forgot that they don't have chimneys here. This is the land of eternal summer.

SANTACLOS
Now you tell me. I had to climb all the way up the roof. It was very slippery. Then I tried to use the door. They have gates...

RUDOLPH
That's to protect themselves from burglars... I'm sorry, Sir. I was so busy... I had so many things to take care of.

SANTACLOS
I know, Rudolph. It's no one's fault. We'll get it right. It's just our first time here. Things don't run smoothly the first time around.

RUDOLPH
What do we do now?

SANTACLOS
We'll find an open window or door.

Someone shines a light upon them.

POLICEMAN *shouts*
¡Alto ahí o disparo!

SANTACLOS
What?

RUDOLPH
He says, "Stop right there or I'll shoot."

The POLICEMAN comes into the scene, gun in hand.

POLICEMAN
¡Manos arriba! Los tenemos rodeados.

SANTACLOS
What now?

RUDOLPH
He says to put our hands up. We're surrounded.

POLICEMAN
¿Dónde está el material?

SANTACLOS
What is he saying?

RUDOLPH *to the Policeman*
Hable despacio, por favor. Sólo un poco de español.

SANTACLOS
Repeat, *por favor.*

POLICEMAN *looking around, finding the sack*
OK. *Un poco de* English... There it is. Put the sack on the floor, very slowly. You do anything funny you're dead.

SANTACLOS
I can't do that. It's going to get wet. What will the children say?

RUDOLPH *to the POLICEMAN*
What's this about?

POLICEMAN
You shut up. I am the law.

RUDOLPH *to SANTACLOS*
I think you better do what he says, Sir. He is the law.

POLICEMAN
Where are the others? Running is no good. The area is full of police.

RUDOLPH
We're surrounded?

SANTACLOS
Why?

POLICEMAN *opens the sack*
And here is the stuff, *un buen cargamento*, ah?

RUDOLPH
Cargamento... Carga...? Cargo. Yes.

POLICEMAN
We knew there would be *un cargamento de drogas por aquí.*

RUDOLPH
Drogas? No! This is Santa Claus. These are toys for the children of the island.

POLICEMAN
I'm warning you, stop the joke. This sack is now confiscated.

RUDOLPH
We had an accident.

POLICEMAN
You don't have to tell *me* that.

SANTACLOS
What's he saying?

RUDOLPH
He thinks we're dealing drugs. He says were picking up some *goods*.

SANTACLOS
(To RUDOLPH) Let me handle this.
(To the POLICEMAN) Señor Policeman. I am Santa Claus

POLICEMAN
Of course, and I am *el Pirata Cofresí*.

SANTACLOS
Mucho gusto, Señor Pirata Cofresí.

POLICEMAN
Stop it right there. I said to quit the joke. You don't play around with the law, do you?

RUDOLPH
It's no joke, Sir. This is the real Santa. Look at his clothes, his beard...
The POLICEMAN shines the flashlight on him and inspects him carefully.

RUDOLPH
And I am the main reindeer, Rudolph. *(Points to the horns and red nose.)* Do you remember the song? *(Sings.) Rudolph, the red nosed reindeer, had a very shiny nose...*

POLICEMAN
Any ID on you?

RUDOLPH *to SANTACLOS*
He wants some identification.

SANTACLOS
I never needed any identification before. I don't have a driver's license, no credit cards, no social security...

RUDOLPH *to SANTACLOS*
I know, Sir. Laugh.

SANTACLOS
Are you crazy? He'll shoot me!

RUDOLPH
(To SANTACLOS) No, Sir.
(To the POLICEMAN) His laugh.

SANTACLOS *half-heartedly*
Ho, Ho, Ho!

RUDOLPH
You'll have to do better than that!

SANTACLOS now putting some effort
HO, HO, HO!

RUDOLPH *to the Policeman*
You see? That is Santa Claus' laughter.

POLICEMAN
Let's look at that sack again. (*Inspects it while on guard, pointing to Santaclos and Rudolph.*) I'll be damned! ¡Si es Santaclos de verdad!

RUDOLPH
Yes, he's the real thing.

SANTACLOS
Sí, verdad, verdad! HO, HO, HO, HO! (*Now very enthusiastically.*)

POLICEMAN
OK, that's enough laughter. (*Puts his gun away.*) I see your sleigh is stuck.

RUDOLPH
Yes, can you give us a hand? *Ayuda?*

The POLICEMAN tries to pull the sleigh out but can't.

POLICEMAN
I'm getting back up. (*Exits.*)

RUDOLPH
Thank you, thank you.
(*To SANTACLOS*) He's going to get help.

SANTACLOS
It's so late already. If we don't hurry we won't be able to make all our visits.

RUDOLPH
There's time. We'll make it.

SANTACLOS
I'm drenched in... warm rain. It's like soup. A little too warm for me. This drastic change in weather can make you... (*Sneezes*) sick.

RUDOLPH
Oh, oh, you better take care.

SANTACLOS sneezes with greater strength. Two MASKED MEN enter the stage, gun in hand.

MASKED MAN 1
¡Si se mueven los dejo tiesos!

RUDOLPH *looking it up in the dictionary*
Tiesos, tiesos... Stiff!
(*To SANTACLOS*) I think there is more trouble ahead. We've had lots of adventures so far...

SANTACLOS
I was expecting another kind of adventure... (*Sneezes*)

MASKED MAN 2 *inspecting the sleigh*
You may be in those clothes but I'm no idiot.

SANTACLOS *cheerfully*
I am Santa Claus. I came from the North Pole to bring toys to the children of this island.

MASKED MAN 2
Don't you dare move, fatty, unless you want to kick the bucket.

MASKED MAN 1 *taking the sack*
Here's the goods. Let's go, things are hot around here. Police is on the lookout. It seems they know about the goods. God, this is heavy. I think it's all in here.

SANTACLOS
What are you doing?

MASKED MAN 2
Tell fatty to zip it. This stuff is ours now.

RUDOLPH
Stuff?

MASKED MAN 1
Yes, now no joking around or I'll blow your head off, horns and all.

RUDOLPH touches his horns in distress, and then sneezes.

MASKED MAN 2
Hey, what's the make of this car?

MASKED MAN 1
I think it's a convertible. It looks special.

MASKED MAN 2
Must be a new brand. Looks Japanese. It says *Sleigh* at the back. That's the name of the make I guess.

MASKED MAN 1
We're wasting time. Let's get gone. You two, leg it.

SANTACLOS
What do you want?

MASKED MAN 2
Make a run for it, it's no joke. And if you look back I'll put one in you. Now, hit the road.

RUDOLPH
They mean business, Sir. They want us to beat it. They're taking the sack.

SANTACLOS
I'll take care of this, Rudolph.
(To the MASKED MEN) I'm Santa Claus. HO, HO, HO, HO!

MASKED MAN 1
Shut up! You're making too much noise. Start walking and be quiet or I'll do you in.

RUDOLPH
I don't think it's going to work this time.

MASKED MAN 2
Shoo, shoo, go on, leave!

SANTACLOS and RUDOLPH leave the area with their hands up in the air while having a sneezing fit. The MASKED MEN take the bag with them in the opposite direction and hide behind a bush to inspect it, while looking out for police.

MASKED MAN 1
Check out how much stuff there is.

MASKED MAN 2 inspects the sack
GODDAMMIT!

MASKED MAN 1 jumps startled
What? What is it?

MASKED MAN 2
Toys!

MASKED MAN 1
It can't be. They said they'd leave the stuff around here.

MASKED MAN 2
There's only toys in here.

MASKED MAN 2 keeps looking in the sack. MASKED MAN 1 looks again afterwards.

MASKED MAN 1
It can't be. It can't be. After we spent the whole night waiting, getting all wet. And we missed Pancho's party. It's not fair... not worth it. I'm changing professions. There's no good in this. It's all sacrifice. Risking our lives to end up with a sack of toys. Not worth it... (*Starts crying*).

MASKED MAN 2
Shush, shush. Calm down. Better times are coming. It's Christmas, time to be joyful and happy.

MASKED MAN 1
So much waiting... (*Whines*). What do we do with the toys?

MASKED MAN 2
Leave them there. They're no good.

MASKED MAN 1 *approaches the sleigh*
Do you think this tiny sports car works? (*He gets in and plays around with things.*) It won't start.

MASKED MAN 2
Leave that too, man. This spot is hot. Fatty and his horns must know where the stuff is. They changed it for toys to trick us. We need to catch them. Quick!

MASKED MAN 1
I wanna go home. So much work...

MASKED MAN 2
Come on!

The POLICEMAN comes in.

POLICEMAN
Santaclos, we're back to give you a hand.

MASKED MAN 1
Good God. The police.

MASKED MAN 2
He who fights and runs away, may live to fight another day!

POLICEMAN
Stop!

Lively music comes on to cheer up their race. MASKED MEN run. The POLICEMAN follows. They all go offstage. We hear shots. The lights go out.

POLICEMAN
Stop! Drop the sack!

OTHER VOICES
Whoa, whoa! Don't shoot! We give up.

END OF ACT 2

ACT 3

CHARACTERS
SANTACLOS
RUDOLPH
(5) REINDEER
BALTHAZAR
MELCHIOR
GASPAR

SETTING
Dawn makes its way in the dark, deep blue background. It's a beautiful day. The sun gradually creeps in through the horizon. SANTACLOS rises with it, topping his ascend with an explosion that pushes his sleigh forward. The sun looks like an orange suspended in space. The stage is clear. We are now looking at a valley, near the beach. We hear the waves crashing, and appreciate nature in its virginal state, the exuberant and bright vegetation of the island: enormous and colorful flowers, human-size ferns, trees brimming with fruit, various birds sing. SANTACLOS enters the stage, accompanied by his REINDEER and leaning on them. RUDOLPH provides a chorus to his sneezing. The race has tired him out enormously. He can barely stay on his feet. The REINDEER enjoy the adventure and the view. RUDOLPH is worried about SANTACLOS and tries to impose order onto the mischievous REINDEER. They listen to him briefly but quickly go back to their games, jokes, and running around.

SANTACLOS
Is *that* what the Three Wise Men call an *asalto*?

RUDOLPH
I don't think so. According to the dictionary that word has several meanings. It means "assault" and also "surprise party." We got the first one.

SANTACLOS
That was close. (*Looking at the rising sun.*) Dear me, the sun is coming out and we didn't bring the toys to the kids. They must be waking up now. This is a disaster. What will they say about me when they get up and find their stockings empty?

RUDOLPH
Maybe they don't hang stockings here.

SANTACLOS
Still, they expect me to bring toys, don't they? (*Sneezes.*)

The REINDEER have gone off to eat sea grapes.

RUDOLPH
(*To the REINDEER*) Watch what you're doing over there. We don't need more trouble, you know.

REINDEER 1
But we came here for adventure.

REINDEER 2
Yes, we're having as many adventures as we can.

REINDEER 3
We like it here.

REINDEER 4
These wild grapes are delicious.

REINDEER 5
Do you want some, Rudolph? (*He brings him some.*)

RUDOLPH
No, thank you. I have more important things to take care of. We have to get back our sleigh, our toys... and we have to figure out a way of giving away the toys.

REINDEER 1
Live it up, Rudolph. We are here.

REINDEER 2
We might as well make the best of it.

The REINDEER continue doing somersaults and putting their feet in front of each other to make themselves trip and fall on the sand.

SANTACLOS
Let them play, Rudolph. I would too if I didn't feel so rotten. (*Sneezes*) We have to think fast. Let's see. Where can we find help?

RUDOLPH
I know, Sir. I know who can help us, the Three Wise Men.

SANTACLOS
Yes, that's a good idea. Where can we find the Three Wise Men?

The THREE WISE MEN materialize behind a bush.

MELCHIOR
Did you want to see us?

SANTACLOS *jumps startled*
Oh, hello! Nice meeting you again.

GASPAR
How did it go?

SANTACLOS
Don't ask.

RUDOLPH
We had slight complications.

BALTHAZAR
Did you find your way around all right?

RUDOLPH
We had technical difficulties.

GASPAR
Isn't the island beautiful?

SANTACLOS
To tell you the truth we haven't had time to enjoy it very much.

SANTACLOS and RUDOLPH sneeze at the same time.

MELCHIOR
You caught a cold.

GASPAR
It's the change in temperature.

MELCHIOR
That's no problem. Here. (*Gets a cup out of his sleeve.*)

RUDOLPH
What is this?

BALTHAZAR
It's soursop tea. It cures everything.

SANTACLOS
I never heard of this tea.

MELCHIOR
It's made of soursop leaves, a tree you find in these islands.

SANTACLOS
It doesn't taste bad.

GASPAR
Did you want to see us?

RUDOLPH
Well, yes. We were wondering if... We lost our sleigh. We need it to get back home.

MELCHIOR
And how did it happen?

SANTACLOS
It's a long story. A long and complicated story. It was raining last night... How can it be so nice and clear all of a sudden? It was pouring not long ago.

GASPAR
This is the tropics. It rains now, and seconds later the sun comes out and dries the land again.

SANTACLOS
We didn't bring our raincoats or anything... We didn't dress for this weather. I tried to give away the toys, but could not find the chimneys... A dog chased me.

RUDOLPH
The police stopped us because they thought we were burglars.

SANTACLOS
Then the burglars took out toys and forced us to go... what are the kids going to say? They'll think I'm an irresponsible fool.

BALTHAZAR
Well, everybody has problems every once in a while.

SANTACLOS
But I'm not used to this. I have my reputation to think of. I never had these kind of problems before. I don't know why it happened in this island.

MELCHIOR
Well, we've had our problems, too. But we have experience here. We know the people.

GASPAR
Believe me, it is not the island's fault. You weren't prepared for it.

SANTACLOS
It's too late now. I lost my opportunity this year.

RUDOLPH
I think we better go home and relax a little. And start to get ready for next year.

SANTACLOS
It is a good thing that we left the island to visit last. Otherwise we would have been in trouble all over the world.

MELCHIOR
How can we help you?

RUDOLPH
First, we must get our sleigh back.

SANTACLOS
It is going to be difficult locating it. It was so dark and we must have run miles and miles.

GASPAR
It's no trouble at all.

The THREE WISE MEN put their arms around each other's shoulders, making a circle. Looking very focused, they utter some unintelligible words. The sounds of the sea become louder. We hear bells and the sleigh flies into the stage. The REINDEER are enjoying the adventurous scene. The sleigh comes down and lands at the center of the stage.

REINDEER 1
Far out.

REINDEER 2
That's pretty neat.

RUDOLPH *inspecting the sleigh*
Yes, this is it. And it's nice and clean, too.

SANTACLOS
Thank you, Wise Men. I can do that trick, too. Only I'm so tired now. But if I could concentrate on it. I'm afraid I'm a little out of shape. I can't think too well in this heat. But if you come to my place again, I can show you all the things I can do. I have a very good aim, too. I throw the toys as I pass above the houses, and they fall into the chimneys, and into the stockings. But here, I don't know what happened.

RUDOLPH
(To SANTACLOS) You need a rest, Sir. That's all. We all need a rest.

The REINDEER have kept playing and eating fruit. Some of them approached the THREE WISE MEN to greet them.

RUDOLPH
(To the REINDEER) O.K., guys. Time to go. You know, this time you better pay more attention to what you're doing. We spent a lot of time training you to pull this sleigh, and your distraction caused the accident. If you don't shape up, we'll have to get new trainees. Please, start taking your positions. We're leaving.
(To Santaclos) Are you ready, Sir?

SANTACLOS
(To RUDOLPH) I guess I am.
(To the THREE WISE MEN) Thank you again, gentlemen. Thank you. *(He gets in the sleigh.)*

RUDOLPH
Thank you very much. *(He takes his position, in front of all the other reindeer.)*

(5) REINDEER *in unison*
Thank you very much.

SANTACLOS
You know, I think your tea worked. I feel better already.

RUDOLPH
Me... (*He starts sneezing but the sneeze never happens.*) too.

SANTACLOS *practices an imperfect laugh*
HO, HO, HO

(5) REINDEER
He, he, he, he.

RUDOLPH gives them a scolding look.

RUDOLPH
(*To SANTACLOS*) You'll get it back, Sir.

SANTACLOS
I hope so. You know, Rudolph, I think that for our next visit we can work out a few changes. Maybe we'll feel more comfortable and will be able to move around better if next year we bring snow to the island. I have good friends in the weather bureau. We can make it snow here, and then our sleigh will slide better, and we can bring winter coats to all the kids. They will love it.

RUDOLPH *not entirely convinced*
That's a possibility. By then I'll know perfect Spanish. I'll be fully bilingual.

GASPAR
So you're planning to come back.

SANTACLOS
We're going home now to get ready for next year. We'll have it figured out by then. We like the island.

(5) REINDEER *in unison*
Yes, yes.

SANTACLOS
We want to come back again and again.

(5) REINDEER *in unison*
Yes, yes.

SANTACLOS
We had some problems this time, but you can't win them all. Next year we will be better, and it should compensate.

RUDOLPH
Yes, these bummers happen everywhere. We know what to expect now. I'll wear my shorts next time.

SANTACLOS
Good-bye, gentlemen.

RUDOLPH
Thank you.

Led by RUDOLPH, the REINDEER pull on the sleigh. The THREE WISE MEN smile while waving good-bye. They stare at the sleigh as it disappears among the clouds. They continue smiling and waving, until we hear a loud explosion. A golden shower sprays the audience. The sun has completely risen.

MELCHIOR
I think the day has exploded.

BALTHAZAR
Sunshine is here!

GASPAR
We should work a little, plan our tour.

The THREE WISE MEN magically get out maps of the island and letters from children.

GASPAR
How about we take the west coast first? Aguada, Mayagüez, down to Ponce, Salinas, up to Fajardo, then Caguas...

MELCHIOR
Let's not forget about the children in Vieques and Culebra.

BALTHAZAR
How about we surprise the children in New York?

GASPAR and MELCHIOR
Excellent idea!

BALTHAZAR *sharing out the letters*
Each one of you, read. Here's one from Rosita in Caguas.

MELCHIOR
Luisito wrote to us.

GASPAR
Luisito from *Buen Consejo*?

MELCHIOR
That's him. Such a good kid.

GASPAR
Here's one from Yvette. She's moved to *Barrio Obrero*.

BALTHAZAR
We forgot something!

GASPAR
What?

BALTHAZAR
What happened to Santaclos' toys?

GASPAR
You're right. They must be lying around somewhere.

MELCHIOR
Let's locate them.

*The THREE WISE MEN throw their arms around each other's shoulders, making a
circle. They focus and utter some unintelligible words. The sack falls from the sky.*

MELCHIOR
Ha! Here they are.

GASPAR
What should we do with them?

MELCHIOR
It'd be a pity they go to waste.

BALTHAZAR
We should get them to their real owners, the kids.

GASPAR
We should consult them, don't you think?

*The THREE WISE MEN address the children in the audience to ask about what they
should do.*

MELCHIOR
Do you think we should return them to Santaclos?

GASPAR
Do you think we should do him a favor and distribute them throughout Borinken for him?

BALTHAZAR
Do you think we should share them with the kids who are here today? And give out
some new toys to the children of Borinken on Epiphany?

*The THREE WISE MEN opt for this last option. They give away the toys among the
children in the audience. In the background, a song begins.[1] The sun above the stage
opens its eyes and smiles. The lyrics to the song appear on the sky (so that children can
sing it). Once they've given all the toys away, the THREE WISE MEN disappear behind
a cloud of smoke.*

---

[1] For tune references, the song here translated is the Puerto Rican aguinaldo (carol) "De tierra lejana."

FROM A LAND AFAR

From a land afar we came to be near you
A star from the East we followed here to see you

Chorus:
Oh thee shining star who the dawn announces
May we never miss your light in the darkness
Glory in all its might to the son of God
Glory in all its might, earth now has his love

A newborn is here, the king of all kings
Gold we bring to him to adorn his wreath

(Chorus)

Godly is this child, we gift him frankincense
Heavenly and warm, so much like his presence

(Chorus)

He came from above to this land of ours
We gift him this myrrh, let's forget our sorrows

(Chorus)

END OF PLAY

UNDECIDED, FROM CAYEY (1979)

CHARACTERS
CLARA, in her mid twenties
RADIO HOST, Mr. Velázquez, only heard in voiceover
MIGUELITO, in his mid twenties, corpulent man
SICO, in his late twenties, Clara's husband
Sico and Clara's NEIGHBORS, a married couple in their mid forties

We hear sweet organ music and the voice of the radio host emerge from the darkness. The stage becomes brighter as the RADIO HOST speaks. CLARA is in her living-dining room. Her modest house is in a small barrio in mountainous Cayey. Highly visible on the dining table sits a portable radio.

RADIO HOST
And to continue with tonight's show, we'll read a letter from one of our listeners.

CLARA puts the volume up. In the kitchen, she checks on the food she's just prepared one last time, and turns off the plates. She shaves her armpits in front of a hand mirror, and then hangs it back on the wall. She stops to listen carefully.

RADIO HOST
It reads like this:

"Dear Mr. Velazquez,

You don't know how many times I've tried to write this letter to tell you about the difficult situation that fills me with doubt and misfortune. I'm a dedicated housewife, somewhat attractive, married to a man who has little trust in me. We've been married for three years. Past our first six months as a married couple, my husband began to change. He gets home with a bad temper; he thinks everything around the house has been done wrong; sometimes he throws a tantrum and leaves to go drink with his friends, arriving then very late at night. He doesn't want me to work. He says as long as he's alive and healthy he'll be in charge of what is every man's duty. When I ask him to let me get a job at the nearby rug factory he says' he doesn't want his wife to work in a place like that, full of lowlifes and deceitful men. Women are even more so, he says, because they spend their days gossiping. These discussions have become physical, despite the fact that I try not to contradict him. I think he would be capable of killing me in one of those episodes.

His lack of consideration and abuse has made me feel cold towards him. Now it is difficult to put up with his touch when he tries to make peace in order to get me into bed. I know that, as his wife, I have the obligation to satisfy my husband's needs, but all the love I had for him has withered with each blow. Sometimes I think about leaving him, and going somewhere where I won't know a thing about him, but where? I wouldn't stay in this town because here divorced women run into a lot of trouble. Besides, when I married him I made a commitment before God and men, and the Bible is my witness.

Sometimes he comes back with gifts, but the following day he leaves again to play pool and drink with his friends until late at night. He spends more time with them than with me. I stay here by myself, listening to your program, which brings such solace to suffering souls. Only God knows why he's put this life's hardships on our way. Should I break my family? Risk him killing me? Where would I go? How do I even begin to put together the pieces of myself in a new place, among strangers? Please, give me your advice.

Awaiting for enlightenment,

Kind regards,

Undecided, from Cayey"

CLARA has repeated the RADIO HOST's words –the final questions and farewell– one by one, in unison. She comes closer to the radio and listens attentively.

RADIO HOST
Dear *Undecided* from Cayey, in hard times, like the ones we live in, when a lack of empathy and violence rule even in the most remote areas of our country, we must be calm and collected when thinking things through; calm and collected.

CLARA
Calm and collected. That's not so easy to do when someone's beating you up...

RADIO HOST
Before making a decision you might later regret, have you asked the Almighty for faith and strength? He sometimes puts difficult tests on our way.

CLARA
Yes, I've asked Him: prayers, candles, I've made promises. But nothing so far.

RADIO HOST
Have you tried talking to your husband at times when he's not agitated, or tired from work?

CLARA
Yes, but he says he doesn't want to talk about the issue.

RADIO HOST
What's the tone of your voice? What's your attitude when you explain to him what's happening to you?

CLARA
Well, I speak naturally, no shouting or anything... But he interrupts me, saying I always nag about the same old thing. He tells me to shut up.

RADIO HOST
Marriage is a sacred bond...

CLARA
Yes, I know...

RADIO HOST
There are times when we have to confront the situation, unshrinking, not try to run away from them, because you can't run away from yourself. And what God has joined together, man must not separate.

CLARA
Well, and what's your advice then?

RADIO HOST
My advice is to think carefully, and much prayer. Have a friendly conversation with your husband, and try to save your marriage by any means possible.

CLARA
I've done all that.

Disheartened, trying to take in the advice, CLARA's sight fixes on the radio but she does not pay attention to the HOST's farewell.

RADIO HOST
And that's it for tonight's show, dear listeners. We hope you've enjoyed our music for those souls in love, our poetry for those souls in wait, and our advice for those hearts in the darkness. This is your friend, Johnny Velazquez, wishing you peace and love. Tune in same time tomorrow for another *Just for you, ladies* show.

Organ music plays. Loud knocking on the door. CLARA turns the radio off in a start. There is knocking again. She remains still and on alert. There is a third knock, she answers.

CLARA
(*Suspicious*) Who is it?

Voice of MIGUELITO
Does Sico live here? Francisco Lopez?

CLARA
He's not home.

MIGUELITO
You're Clara, right? Sico has told me about you.

CLARA
Sico is not home. He may be at Domingo's bar. Look for him there.

MIGUELITO
I'm an old friend of Sico's. I came by foot from downtown. I wouldn't want to leave without seeing him...

CLARA
(*Somewhat annoyed by his insistence*) I already told you Fico is not home.

MIGUELITO
Excuse me, would you be so kind as to give me a glass of water?

CLARA *hesitating*
Well, wait, I'll bring you some. (*Gets water from the kitchen and cautiously opens the door.*) I don't know what time he'll be back...

MIGUELITO lets himself in before she gets a chance to say anything about it and takes the glass of water.

MIGUELITO
So, you are Clara. Nice to meet you. (*He shakes her hand vigorously.*) Sico has told me so much about you. (*He moves in and takes a seat.*) Can I have a seat? I've walked a lot. You gotta shift into first gear to go up that hill, don't you? I imagine you go up it everyday.

CLARA
Well, I'm used to it. (*Takes the empty glass from Miguelito's hand.*) Sir, I really don't know when Sico will be back.

MIGUELITO
Sico, Sico, what a guy! He talks so much about you.

CLARA
About me?

MIGUELITO
Yes, he says you're a beautiful woman, hard working, a good housewife.

CLARA
Sico says that?

MIGUELITO
Yes, and that your cooking is delicious.

CLARA
Sico... He likes to talk.

MIGUELITO *aware of Clara's discomfort*
Sico and I have been friends for a long time. We were almost kids still. We were buddies in the army. Such a great guy. Does he still like to bet at the cockfights, and to crack a joke?

CLARA nods without saying a word. She is quietly examining him.

CLARA
Sir, I'm sure if you go to that bar on the way out of town, the one called *Morir Soñando*, you'll find him there.

MIGUELITO
He must be about to arrive, right?

CLARA
It's difficult to say. It depends on whether he loses at pool too many times, if he gets stubborn and loses his temper. He could be back at eleven, or at one o'clock in the morning...

MIGUELITO
I'll wait here a few minutes, okay? I'll be leaving for New York as soon as tomorrow, that's where I live, and so I won't be able to see him if I don't see him tonight. Where you about to go to bed?

CLARA
Honestly, yes, I was.

MIGUELITO
Well, if you want, I can wait outside... on the balcony.

CLARA
Sico has never talked to me about you.

MIGUELITO
My goodness! Sico's always so reserved. He always says friends and family don't mix, because friends are the ones we really open up to. Isn't that something? Friends know you better than your wife or your kids. Do you have any kids?

CLARA
No.

MIGUELITO
You see, when men get together with their friends to drink, and play, and talk, that's when the important things come up. There are things you can't talk about with women. You get me?

CLARA
Yes. And women have things they can't talk about with men.

MIGUELITO
Men are men, and they get each other.

CLARA
I don't get what you're saying. Some men are different, right? Each one of us is different. Some people talk more with their families, and some talk less. In Sico's case, I know once he's had a few he gets talking about personal stuff. But there are other

men who talk about the things they see and what happens to them, at home with their wives.

We hear a noise coming from the patio. MIGUELITO jumps up.

MIGUELITO
What was that?

CLARA
The neighbor's dog. He plays with the trash at night. (*Pauses.*) Well, I...

MIGUELITO *gathering his composure*
I had pictured you much older.

CLARA
Must be the way Sico speaks about me. He's always spotting the flaws.

MIGUELITO
But you're young and beautiful. You don't look like a married woman.

CLARA
Well, I have been for three years.

MIGUELITO *in a playful tone*
Did you have many suitors before getting married?

CLARA *offended*
No, sir, I did not. Sico was my first boyfriend. My family is very strict. My mom is a Jehovah's Witness; she raised us by the Bible.

MIGUELITO
Do you believe in the Bible?

CLARA
Well, some things in it. Others, I don't understand.

MIGUELITO *gets up and puts his body on display*
Sico must have grown a belly by now, didn't he?

CLARA *nervous, paying attention to the man's movements*
He's always been a bit... He's left himself fatten up a bit. Well, yes, it's been a year since...

MIGUELITO
You, on the contrary, have kept yourself thin, young, in good shape...

CLARA
Have you had dinner? I made a codfish soup for Sico. There is enough for you, if you'd like some...

MIGUELITO
I haven't had a bite to eat the whole day. That would suit me. Plus, if you're as good a cook as Sico makes you out to be, I must try that soup.

On her way to the kitchen, CLARA stops at the mirror for a second and fixes a lose hair with a swift motion.

MIGUELITO
Clara, have you been to New York?

CLARA *taken aback by his sudden overtly friendly tone*
Never. I don't think I would like the cold, although I would like to see snow.

CLARA puts the bowl on the table. MIGUELITO sits down. While he eats, she begins to mend one of Sico's shirts.

MIGUELITO
Snow looks very beautiful on postcards and calendars, but with people squelching, and the cars in the city it all turns to mush, just like when it rains here.

CLARA
There is a lot of crime over there.

MIGUELITO
Over here, too. It's the same everywhere. This soup is good. (*He moves the bowl away.*) You cook even better than Sico said.

CLARA
Anyone knows how to make a codfish soup. It's the easiest thing in the world.

MIGUELITO *getting up*
Not this good. You look very good too.

MIGUELITO moves closer to her. CLARA moves her mending materials aside and, startled, gets up.

CLARA
Stop that. Don't you talk to me like that. Sico...

MIGUELITO
Sico is not here.

CLARA
That doesn't matter. It's not because of Sico. It's because of me.

MIGUELITO
Don't be mad. Sico and I talk about women like that. What's wrong with telling a woman she looks good. I'm very frank, that's all.

CLARA
So am I. and I'm telling you to stop it with that tone. I don't like it.

MIGUELITO
You have your temper too.

CLARA
You're finished with your soup, right? Look, Sico might take a while. It's better that you go find him.

MIGUELITO
I found what I was looking for, Clarita.

MIGUELITO moves closer to her and holds her by the arm. She sets herself free.

CLARA
What's up with you? Look, sir, you better leave right now.

MIGUELITO
What is Sico going to say? That you kick his friends out of his house.

CLARA
A friend would not do what you've done.

MIGUELITO
And what did I do, sweety?

MIGUELITO turns the radio on. We hear salsa music.

CLARA
Look, stop it with the overt friendliness. Go, leave me alone.

CLARA heads towards the door. MIGUELITO grabs hold of her by her wrists.

CLARA
Let go of me!

MIGUELITO
I know what you need, *mami*.

They struggle.

MIGUELITO
Your husband gave me the clues to come get you. I went into the bar on that little hill. Your husband was paying everyone a round since he'd won at the numbers. We got talking about women: that they like to suffer, that they like men to mistreat them, that that's what his wife was like, who was home alone, waiting for him to get home... I was curious to meet you.

CLARA makes a bigger effort to set herself free. She tries to scream. MIGUELITO covers her mouth with his hand. She bites it. He hits her on the face. She falls down. He sexually attacks her on the floor. We hear SICO's voice, singing as he approaches the house.

SICO'S VOICE
One should never tell a woman how much you love her, because it's very difficult to understand a woman's heart...

MIGUELITO leaves her on the floor and leaves in a rush through the back door. SICO fiddles with the front door.

SICO *yelling*
Open the door, damn it! Why did you lock it from the inside?

CLARA sits up. SICO shoves himself in.

SICO
What's going on here?

CLARA starts crying. In tears, she finishes gathering herself up. She fixes her hair. She smooths out her dress, now torn. She turns the radio off.

CLARA
It's your fault. You started talking about me at the bar. That son of a bitch came because you sent him here.

SICO
What are you talking about?

CLARA
About the guy who came here, damn it. He hit me and...

SICO
Here? And how did he get in?

CLARA
I opened the door because he said he was a friend of yours. He knew my name and yours. He heard you talking at Domingo's bar.

SICO
I've told you not to open the door, not even if Christ himself comes here.

CLARA
He asked for water. He said you went to the army together, that he'd made a long trip to come see you, that he had to leave for New York right away...

SICO
And what did he do to you?

CLARA *dubious, on the alert for SICO's reaction*
He grabbed me by the arm...

SICO
What else?

CLARA
He told me he had found what he was looking for. I told him to leave.

SICO
But get to the point, damn it. Did he..?

CLARA
I told him not to talk to me with that tone...

SICO
But did he get to...?

CLARA
No, damn it. He didn't get to. He didn't. He didn't.

SICO *scatterbrained because of the alcohol and the news*
I've told you a thousand times not to talk to men you don't know. What are people going to think about me when they find out about this? They'll say I'm a cuckold, that you incited him and got him into the house. (*Losing strength.*) Why does this happen to me, damn it? What will people think? How will I face them?

CLARA *fierce, takes a leap with a knife on her hand*
It's your fault, you asshole. You son of a bitch.

CLARA wounds him. SICO draws back with a scream. He collapses. CLARA looks at him terrified for an instant.

CLARA *exits the house running and yells*
Help, anyone! For the love of God, Sico is dead.

SICO *sits up and mumbles*
Asshole. After I paid for your drinks, you son of a bitch... you'll pay for this one. And you, letting into the house any guy that comes by. You whore!

CLARA enters the house, followed by the NEIGHBORS.

CLARA
You're alive!

The NEIGHBORS come closer to examine the wound.

SICO
No, it wasn't a fatal one. No one's killing me. And whoever tries will get the worst of me, damn it.

MALE NEIGHBOR
But what happened? Who wounded you?

CLARA and SICO exchange a tense and quick look.

CLARA
It was...

SICO
Nothing. It was nothing. Some motherfucker mugged me on my way back. He wanted my money. It looks like he knew I had won at the numbers today... He stabbed me in the darkness, but he couldn't kill me.

FEMALE NEIGHBOR
But where was this? I heard you singing as you passed by our house...

SICO *confused*
Ehh, it was here... almost here...

MALE NEIGHBOR
Did you manage to see him?

SICO
It was very dark, but I saw him. He's not from around here.

FEMALE NEIGHBOR
How about you, Clara? Did you manage to see him?

CLARA
I...

SICO
No, she didn't. She was inside. It was all very quick.

MALE NEIGHBOR
Let's get to the hospital, Sico, quick.

SICO
Nah, never mind. This will heal by itself.

FEMALE NEIGHBOR
But Sico, it could get infected.

SICO

Come on, come on. It's not a big deal. I've had worse. But that motherfucker better be careful. I'll be looking for him under every rock. He'll pay for this, damn it. (*Pauses.*) Would you like something to eat? Clara, get them something...

MALE NEIGHBOR

No, Sico, it's late. We were asleep. We came over because Clara said you were hurt. We thought...

SICO

You know how women exaggerate things.

FEMALE NEIGHBOR

Someone should call the police.

SICO

None of that. For what? What will they do that I can't do myself?

FEMALE NEIGHBOR

However you put it, there's a criminal on the loose.

SICO

There's many of them. Anyway, what's the police going to do? Questions, and more questions, reports, and nonsense.

MALE NEIGHBOR

Well, we'll be on our way then.

SICO

Be careful out there.

The NEIGHBORS exit. CLARA walks them quietly to the door.

SICO

Be careful with what you find out there.

CLARA

...

SICO

Tomorrow I'm putting a lock on the outside of this damn house, and some metal bars.

CLARA
That won't be necessary.

CLARA begins to put some clothes in a paper bag.

SICO
What are you doing?

CLARA
What you see. I know what I have to do. The rest is your problem. Do whatever you feel like doing. Tell whatever story you like.

SICO
Are you crazy? Where do you think you're going this late at night? You're not going anywhere.

CLARA
Where I go is none of your business. I'm none of your business anymore.

SICO tries to hold her by the arm.

CLARA *with absolute self-control*
You put a finger on me and I'll kill you, motherfucker.

SICO steps back, shocked by her strength. CLARA takes her bag full of clothes. When she makes it to the door she goes back in, goes to the table where the radio is and puts in the bag. She looks at SICO defiantly one last time. She exits with decisiveness. SICO fades out in the darkness.

END OF PLAY

DON'T GET NERVOUS
(1975)

(Two interludes)

FIRST INTERLUDE

CHARACTERS
MAN
VICENTE, his best friend

MAN
Don't get nervous. Let's pause.

VICENTE
Don't think much of my questions.

MAN
(*To the audience*) Pauses, great silences, spaces between words are more difficult. Out there horns honk on Third Avenue. They hit you with a sound foreign to your body, and have the impact of an overturned truck.

VICENTE
Why do you look at me like that?

MAN
(*To the audience*) I have the bad habit of staring at people.

VICENTE
I get the impression you're analyzing me, laughing at me on the inside. I don't like that. After the confession it'll be more difficult for me to be your friend because I know you better.

MAN
(*To VICENTE*) Now you're the one doing the analyzing. I told you who I am because I feel something great for you.

(*To the audience*) It sounds strange when a man says *he loves you* with a cracking voice. (*To VICENTE*) I don't mind if you bolt out that door and I never see you again.

VICENTE
'Nother drink?

MAN
(*To himself*) You see him get up, his short moves making him minute. He's something else. He must be your guardian angel...

> My Guardian dear,
> To whom God's love commits me here,
> Over this night be at my side.

...The one on your First Communion certificate. The ice sings as it tumbles in the glass. At the end of the arm that hands you the drink there's his effort to smile. Vicente has been your best friend for a long time: the hands that opened your way, a pillow to your body, the food in your belly.
(*To VICENTE*) The rain looks like thin snow.

VICENTE
(*To himself*) Look at him. He talks like you. He doesn't draw his eyebrows. He doesn't wave his hands around like other fags you see. I can't feel my hands. He even looks at peace. He loves you. Why you? A good friend, yes, but that's not your thing. You didn't get up. You don't get up. Aren't you thinking of bolting out the door?
(*To MAN*) May I sit here?

MAN
(*To VICENTE*) Look, don't start with formalities. The best thing to do is to act normal, as if nothing's been said.
(*To audience*) One can do anything as long as it's not put into words. It can all have different names.
(*To VICENTE*) After all, we're friends.

VICENTE
I don't care what you are. That's a thing aside, secondary.

MAN
(*To himself*) You realize there's something in his eyes. It may be the alcohol. This guy is melting. Now that he's looked at you to inject himself in you, you can't stop the energy that spreads around, touching your face: you feel your beard warming up.

You say...

(*To VICENTE*) Smile, man. I'm used to seeing you smile, to seeing you making me smile, to laughing with you.

(*To himself*) You feel a head on the palm of your hand. It's fallen from so high: ripe breadfruit, a stone turned into ripples in the water. Someone calls your name. Someone gets inside your name and opens it from within. As if it were a little five-cent surprise box, inside, there are five candies wrapped in colorful waxed paper, and a frog-shaped whistle. Someone spills. You tremble. The water is up to your waist. It drags you. *Close your eyes and open your mouth. Tag, you're it. Cold, cold, colder; warm, hot, boiling.* You can't escape his eyes now. Smile to let him know it's all cool. You join your two halves, kiss *your* lips, make *your* face closer to your cheekbones by putting your hands over *your* shoulders. You find yourself in the circles of *your* eyes. You see a nervous hand turn off the lights and call you. There's a tree growing on the roof, it offers guavas and those twin guineps you avidly search for in the bunch you just bought. Your body repeats itself a thousand times and more because the bed sheet spreads over an abyss.

(*To VICENTE*) Don't say my name.

VICENTE

(*To himself*) I'll copy you. I'll put carbon paper between our bodies.

(*To Man*) You're hot.

MAN

(*To himself*) You're sweating, and the sweat is twice as much, twice the saliva, twice the breathing.

VICENTE

(*To MAN*) I would have liked for this ceiling to not be made of glass.

(*To himself*) My lips and their imminent quiver. An energy moves all over your chest, kisses your testicles, crushes you with a death wish.

MAN

(*To himself*) While you slide down a gutter in which gravity rules, the trees passing by seek out your breath. Angels in a translucent purple light guide minotaurs who scatter seeds near trees that grow only to fasten to your waist and lift you up. So many trees asking for rain make it impossible to walk. They want rain and birds. Their branches impose on you to make you grow. Each electric leaf soaks up your sap. (*To VICENTE*) Vicente, give me rain.

VICENTE
(*To himself*) Dark clouds speeding by cover up the sky.

MAN
(*To himself*) Thick rain slowly falls upon the trees.
(*To the audience*) He takes a deep breath and lets it out abruptly one last time. He hands me the towel.

VICENTE
I'm cold.

MAN
Wear your body then.

VICENTE
Which one's mine?

MAN
Either one. Are you sleepy?

VICENTE
A little.

MAN
It's the drinks, man.

VICENTE
My head's spinning like a top.

MAN
Then go to sleep.

END OF FIRST INTERLUDE

SECOND INTERLUDE

CHARACTERS
MONCHO
WOMAN
NEIGHBORS

MONCHO
You sharpened the knife and gave yourself time to change your mind, but you killed her anyway. Over your eyes, the frames of a film full of adventure, passion, mystery...
     Time has stopped because I don't want to think about the future. I won't try to escape when they cuff me and take me to the police patrol, having to make way for me amidst onlookers lining the street.

NEIGHBOR 1
Moncho was a hard-working man, decent.

NEIGHBOR 2
He never raised his voice.

NEIGHBOR 3
He didn't have any enemies.

NEIGHBOR 4
He'd always stop by and talk to people.

NEIGHBOR 5
He'd always have a joke to tell.

NEIGHBOR 6
Like a "joke of the day" that he'd bring to work, share with neighbors and family.

MONCHO
My life came to an end the precise moment the knife broke into her silky skin and ribs, when the blood streamed down my shirt, when her warmth escaped through the holes the knife made. It ended with her three screams, the last one choked up, with her nails clawing on my wrist —her last touch—, with her last look, her eyes begging as I leaned over her face to take it in and make it mine, and keep it in my memory like a photograph dedicated to me.
     When you first spotted her dancing she gave you such a leg show you had to look at her face.

The first thing I look at in a chick is her legs. I don't like skinny legs. I like to see little hairs under the nylons.

What scared you was the way she looked at you, with such confidence you had to look away. You felt weird because she was winning right from the beginning. On that first battle, she conquered you with a look.

Right from the beginning, I knew I had to find an excuse to talk to her. She beat me to it.

WOMAN
You're new here, right? Are you Chegüi's cousin? You look a lot like him. How long will you be staying here? You got a job? Winter is around the corner. The first one's always the hardest to put up with, but you'll get used to it. I like changing seasons. Your clothes, your activities, even your personality changes. One is born anew with each season, or at least you can pretend you're different. Life repeats itself every year: from caterpillar to butterfly, and from butterfly to caterpillar. When I put on last year's coat, it's as if a series of memories came with it because they're part of the coat. Bodies come back to life in April, but I see you're not interested in this conversation... Me? Ten years ago. Yes, I speak it well because I always practice. My family speaks it at home. My mom's from Ciales, the countryside, and never bothered to learn English. She says she's too old for that. She didn't need it either. She watches TV in Spanish, listens to the radio in Spanish, she prays in Spanish, she shops at the *bodega* around the corner, and the floor lady at the factory where she worked was *boricua*.

MONCHO
(*To himself*) That voice, Moncho, is gone forever. Your knife ended that hot voice that came out in a sigh, a little hoarse, as if she were always telling a secret, Moncho. (*To WOMAN*) Stop. Stop it, girl. I can't control myself. You drive me crazy kissing me like that, and I can't find a way to stop, and I could even do something stupid.

WOMAN
Moncho, I love you so much. I want to spend my life with you.

MONCHO
What are you saying? Of course, you're going to be my woman.

WOMAN
No, not your woman. I'm going to share everything with you, but I'm not going to be your property.

MONCHO
That's O.K. I'm not saying you'll be my property. I want the best for you, that's why I want to respect you until marriage. I respect you too much to sleep with you before our wedding. I'd rather sleep with a woman of the night and deal her a blow than tarnish you.

WOMAN
And what am I supposed to do? Get a man of the night?

MONCHO
(*To WOMAN*) You think everything's a joke.
(*To himself*) Moncho, did you realize she made a face when you said that? You found out about the truth much later, by the time you were already seeing her face on the faces of every other woman on the street, on the subway, on the warehouse where you do the inventory, on the Playboy magazines, on the cigarette ads, by the time you had to see her every night in order to sleep. And so in the afternoons, once work was over, you'd run to take a shower, then up five flights of steps like a rocketship, panting when she showed herself behind that door. Her mother would ask if you wanted coffee, you'd say yes and she'd get up to prepare it once the soap opera went to ads. That was when she was running a bit late and still taking a shower when you arrived. Her old woman was very quiet and would sit in front of the TV, stupefied by the soap opera.

WOMAN
Moncho, I work too. You think I spend my days lazing around the house? Sometimes I'm a bit late: the subway, the bus, I'm tired, dunno... You have to trust me. I really love you, I miss you, I want to be with you. I too have dreams, plans, desires. I'm not a little girl who needs your protection. We both need protection. No, no, no, you don't get it. That has nothing to do with love. I love you, I miss you so much, but I can't see you acting like the boss of me, watching over my every step.

MONCHO
You did well, Moncho, not letting her finish her sentence. She's used to being the boss and she's going to want to wear the pants around the house. You'll become the laughingstock of the whole town. Yes, you will, because as soon as you marry they'll say, "Look at that motherfucker, all dominated by his wife." I don't mean you want to be a dictator, but the man is the man, and the man's the one who makes the decisions: whether she can dye her hair or cut it, or take a job out there, or dance with another man, or go to the movies with her girlfriends. You're not making that up. Everybody knows that's how things work. That's normal, Moncho, it's decent.
        Her eyes and mouth are halfway open. Dry blood has made her hair a sticky wad; her breasts are uncovered.
(*To WOMAN*) Let's get married, girl. I crave for you so much each day is a struggle to not jump on you and enjoy you to the end, ten times a night, every night.

WOMAN
Why don't you say, "and enjoy each other to the end"? I want to enjoy you too, feel you inside me, writhe and moan with pleasure.

MONCHO
(*To himself*) She speaks like a whore, Moncho, as if she knew a lot about those things, as if she'd slept with a lot of men.
(*To WOMAN*) You speak as if you've had a lot of experience in the matter.

WOMAN
No, Moncho, I don't have that much experience, but a woman knows what she wants, even when she's never had it, and she can imagine the pleasure, and she can get randy thinking about those things like any man does. The only difference is you can talk about those things while we can't.

MONCHO
(*To himself*) That's true, Moncho, but it won't stop you fretting about it, will it? Because it's hard to trust a woman who speaks about those things just like that. But you don't care. You'll give her the news about the apartment you rented, and the furniture you bought, and tell her you want to get married as soon as possible. Moncho, you have to stop being so old fashioned, man.
(*To WOMAN*) What's wrong? You're as white as a sheet. I thought you'd be happy to hear that, jumping up and down.

WOMAN
But, I am so happy. But, I have to tell you something, before we go on making plans. I've never lied to you and I don't want to start our marriage off with a lie.

MONCHO
I wonder where that fly went, the one that's been going around your head, whispering things to you, standing on the knife to have a taste of the sticky blood.
 I was going to deal her a blow in the face and beat her to death. But she didn't even deserve that. She cried as she told me the story, but I kept hardening up like a rock and her tears didn't mean anything to me. In a matter of minutes, what I felt for her became a thick hatred that choked up in my throat.

NEIGHBOR 1
You did well, breaking up the engagement and breaking up with her at once. Now go, sell the furniture and leave the apartment, go back to Puerto Rico to forget 'bout all this, 'bout this disgusting city, where women don't know how to be respectful and decent.

MONCHO
But she can't stay unpunished after doing this to me. Taking me for a fool and then stay cool as a cucumber? I swear by my balls this won't stay like this. I can't live with this in my head. I'm a *macho*, damn it. And *machos* deserve respect.

NEIGHBOR 2
Calm down, Moncho. Take it easy. Drop that knife. It's not worth it to end up in jail for a girl like that.

MONCHO
But I can't live at ease thinking about how that whore is sleeping with everyone in town, ridiculing me. People will laugh at me. I will know whenever I step into the barbershop, into the bar, everybody will be looking at me with the corner of their eye. And even if they don't, I'll know. She'll be laughing up her sleeve at me.

WOMAN
Moncho, I hadn't told you before because I didn't know how. It was too difficult to put it into words. That happened a long time ago.

MONCHO
Do you regret it?

WOMAN
No. I loved him, or at least I thought I did. That's why I did it. I was very young and didn't think about what would come after. Then we realized it wasn't working. Moncho, I'm not a woman like that, who goes to bed with anyone who crosses her path. All that happened before we met, and has nothing to do with my feelings for you.

MONCHO
I knew she was coming to the apartment today to get her things. I didn't talk to her when she came in. You could tell she'd been crying all night. But tears wouldn't get me all soft. I realized she was expecting a word from me, but I took the bull by the horns and shut my mouth. Behind her tears I heard a...

WOMAN
I truly love you, Moncho.

MONCHO
The first one was to her stomach. The second one too. It felt as if I were tearing a wool pillow. The other ones kept coming, as if another person was in charge of my hand.

(To WOMAN) I loved you too, but why did you try to fool me?

Now, Moncho. It's standing on your arm. A quick blow and you can kill that fucking fly.

END OF SECOND INTERLUDE

NEWARK, 1974

(an interlude based on the Branch Brook Park Puerto Rican riots)

CHARACTERS
DOLFO
NEIGHBORS
JOSEPH BACKSCRATCHER
PHOTOGRAPHER
CANDY
AURORA TROUBLEMAKER
CRAPSHOOTERS (2)
MAYOR
MOUNTED POLICEMAN
ARMED POLICEMAN

SCENE 1.
Seventh Avenue, Newark. Don Dolfo's Bodega. Don Dolfo is behind the counter, arranging the merchandise. Two female neighbors enter the store.

DOLFO
How may I help you, ladies?

The ladies are still wrapped up in their previous conversation.

FEMALE NEIGHBOR 1
Do you know what happened to Juancito? They hit him at school and came home with a black eye. I don't know what I'm going to do with that kid. I can't send my kids to school with the certainty that they'll come back home safe and sound.

FEMALE NEIGHBOR 2
Yes, that's very true. The best you can do is put ice on it so that the swelling comes down. Last week...

DOLFO
Ladies, how may I help you?

The ladies look at Dolfo.

FEMALE NEIGHBOR 1
Do you have *yautías*?

DOLFO
Yes, ma'am.

FEMALE NEIGHBOR 1
How much?

DOLFO
Seventy-five cents a pound.

FEMALE NEIGHBOR 1
Dolfo, that's so expensive!

DOLFO
All prices have gone up. What do you want me to do?

AURORA TROUBLEMAKER enters. She entertains herself by looking at the magazines and listening into the neighbors' conversation.

FEMALE NEIGHBOR 1
Then give me five pounds of *yautías*, five of plantains, and three of ground meat. I'm going to sell *alcapurrias* at the park tomorrow.

Two MALE NEIGHBORS come in.

MALE NEIGHBOR 1
Dolfo, give me a beer. No, two. Do you want one?

MALE NEIGHBOR 2
Yes.

AURORA
(To FEMALE NEIGHBOR 1) Ma'am, are you thinking of selling food at the park?

FEMALE NEIGHBOR 1
Yes, ma'am. I've always sold my *alcapurrias* at the festival, every year. Everybody sells stuff at the park during the festival. Why wouldn't we Puerto Ricans be able to do it, too?

FEMALE NEIGHBOR 2
And what would a Puerto Rican Festival be without *alcapurrias* and *arroz con gandules*? Dolfo, are you thinking of going tomorrow?

AURORA
A Puerto Rican Festival?

DOLFO
Of course I am. The whole neighborhood's going to be there.

MALE NEIGHBOR 2
I'm taking my whole family. It's rare to be able to go out together to an event like that.

AURORA
There will be important people there. That's why I'm going. Joseph Backscratcher will be speaking tomorrow. That's what I call a community leader! He's running for a position in City Hall. And he'll do a lot of things for the Puerto Rican community if he gets elected. Did you see his picture on the newspaper? He was shown giving a handshake to the mayor.

FEMALE NEIGHBOR 1
I don't trust those political intriguers. They all do the same thing. They promise the community heaven and earth, with cold and hot water...

MALE NEIGHBOR 1
...day care centers...

MALE NEIGHBOR 2
...jobs... But once they're up there...

FEMALE NEIGHBOR 2
...what they care about is not loosing their jobs and making some money.

AURORA
We need more Puerto Ricans in those positions.

FEMALE NEIGHBOR 1
Yes, but we need Puerto Ricans who represent their people, and not their own interests. Otherwise, what does it matter if they're Puerto Rican or not? (*To MALE NEIGHBOR 1*) Hey, are you headed home now?

MALE NEIGHBOR 1
Yes.

FEMALE NEIGHBOR 2
Then give me a hand with these bags. Dolfo, put these on the list.

They all say good-bye and exit on the right. The stage remains in complete darkness.

SCENE 2.

Branch Brook Park Festival. From the darkness, we hear the distant sound of the bongos. The sound becomes louder as the light comes on stage. The NEIGHBORS begin to come in, saying hi, preparing their tables, dancing, and playing their instruments. We can hear the bongos throughout the scene. On the back of the stage, two CRAPSHOOTERS play dice. The stallholders announce their products. JOSEPH BACKSCRATCHER enters. He fixes his microphone and prepares to give his speech. He says hi to some of the neighbors.

BACKSCRATCHER
Check, check, check, one, two, three. Your attention, please. Welcome everyone, to this years' Puerto Rican Cultural Festival. On behalf of the Association for the Betterment of the Hispanic Community of Newark, I want to thank everyone for their participation in this event. I'd also like to thank all the Hispanic merchants for helping us make today's event possible. Special thanks to Don Dolfo from *La Islita Grocery Store* on Seventh Avenue for his cooperation... Before proceeding with today's activities, I'd like to inform you about some things happening within our community that are of great importance, more precisely, that local elections will take place in our city soon. I will be running for City Councilman in these elections and I am here before you asking for the support of the Hispanic community. It is only with your support that I'd be elected as your representative. So please register to vote as soon as possible, and tell your friends and family to register too. Remember: a vote for me is a vote for you. This is the only way we can start to solve all of our problems...

AURORA TROUBLEMAKER applauds enthusiastically.

AURORA
Very good! Very good! That's what we need! Go Backscratcher, go!

The audience is not convinced by his speech and starts to shoot questions at him.

CANDY
Problems, you say? My husband's in jail and he didn't do nothing! What you gonna do to get him out of there?

BACKSCRATCHER
Ah, I don't know... Yes, I know a good lawyer. Stop by my office tomorrow and we'll see what we can do.

FEMALE NEIGHBOR 1
What you gonna do to fix the projects on Seventh Avenue? They're falling apart.

FEMALE NEIGHBOR 2
Yes, those projects are so dirty you have to wear boots to go into the elevators. What you gonna do about that?

BACKSCRATCHER
Eh, eh...

MALE NEIGHBOR 1
Look, when I go to the bathroom to use the toilet, and it's raining outside, I have to go in with an umbrella. How you gonna solve that?

MALE NEIGHBOR 2
Yes, and how about police? They're always around, beating us up, clubbing us down! I assume you're gonna stop that...

BACKSCRATCHER
Well, the police is here to protect you. They represent the law and we must respect them.

FEMALE NEIGHBOR 1
And what you gonna do about the schools? They're not teaching nothing to our kids.

BACKSCRATCHER
That's why we need to organize ourselves as a community. I can't do this alone, but I am willing to represent you.

A press PHOTOGRAPHER enters and goes to BACKSCRATCHER.

PHOTOGRAPHER
Good afternoon, Mr. Backscratcher. I'm from the *Star Ledger* and I would like to take a few pictures of you and your constituents. Would you pose over there?

BACKSCRATCHER
Of course, I would be glad to. It's my pleasure.

AURORA TROUBLEMAKER comes to say hi to him and gives him a handshake at the same time they're taking the picture. The NEIGHBORS comment on her. BACK-SCRATCHER says goodbye and goes talk to the two CRAPSHOOTERS playing dice at the back. Initially, he doesn't realize they're shooting craps.

BACKSCRATCHER *looking at the dice*
Are you registered to vote? (*He looks at the dice.*)

CRAPSHOOTER 1
Yes, yes, we're registered already.

CRAPSHOOTER 1 grabs BACKSCRATCHER by the edge of his pants. They are a bit drunk. Annoyed, BACKSCRATCHER removes the hand from his pants.

BACKSCRATCHER
Remember: a vote for me is a vote for you.

BACKSCRATCHER leaves, goes buy an alcapurria, *and meets AURORA TROUBLE-MAKER again.*

AURORA
Mr. Backscratcher, did you see what those men are doing? It's shameful; it even makes me feel ashamed of being Puerto Rican.

BACKSCRATCHER
Yes, ma'am. I'll fix that right now.

BACKSCRATCHER spots a MOUNTED POLICEMAN patrolling on horseback and walks to him.

BACKSCRATCHER
Mr. Officer, there are two guys shooting craps back there and that looks bad for our community. What are you going to do about it?

MOUNTED POLICEMAN
Yeah, we've already seen them. We're going to break it up now.

BACKSCRATCHER
Would you like a cigarette?

MOUNTED POLICEMAN
No, thanks.

The MOUNTED POLICEMAN makes his way to the CRAPSHOOTERS, breaking through the community on his horse. He rides around them once, then stops. The bongos play harder. Quickly, the COMMUNITY becomes alarmed.

MOUNTED POLICEMAN
What are you guys doing?

One of the CRAPSHOOTERS starts to get up, but before he's finished or says anything the MOUNTED POLICEMAN clubs him on the head. The other CRAPSHOOTER makes a run for it. The MOUNTED POLICEMAN runs after him, riding over a woman with her child. He shoots the runaway, killing him. EVERYONE drops to the floor, trying to hide from the shots, the club blows, and the tear gas, because they've been hit, or because they're trying to help others. While the MOUNTED POLICEMAN slowly turns back towards the crowd, the COMMUNITY begins to stand up in slow motion. Once they're all standing, they throw themselves at the MOUNTED POLICEMAN, who confronts them by shouting and holding his gun in one leap. They all freeze.

SCENE 3.
At the Mayor's office, and in front of City Hall. The confrontation between the COMMUNITY and the POLICEMAN remains a frozen scene. The MAYOR is in his office, waiting for BACKSCRATCHER's arrival. BACKSCRATCHER enters on the right and walks towards the office. When he makes it to the entrance, he's stopped by an ARMED POLICEMAN.

ARMED POLICEMAN *pointing his shotgun at BACKSCRATCHER*
Hold it there.

BACKSCRATCHER
I'm Mr. Backscratcher. I have an appointment with the Mayor.

The ARMED POLICEMAN checks his list.

ARMED POLICEMAN
Oh, yeah, Mr. Backscratcher. Go ahead.

BACKSCRATCHER goes into the Mayor's office.

MAYOR *shaking his hand*
Mr. Buttscratcher...

BACKSCRATCHER
It's *Back*scratcher, *back*.

MAYOR
Yeah, well, anyways, the Puerto Rican community is really uptight. There has been a little disturbance in Branch Brook Park, you know?

BACKSCRATCHER
Yes, Sir, I already know.

MAYOR
I'm going to have to speak to the Puerto Rican community sometime soon... they need to see an authority figure from their own community in order to calm them down. I'm going to need your help.

BACKSCRATCHER
I'm at your disposition, Sir.

MAYOR
They might not understand what I have to tell them. So if things get out of hand, you'll help me calm them down by speaking to them. That always works. You do know how to speak to your community?

BACKSCRATCHER
Yes, Sir, absolutely.

MAYOR
Well, let's go. I'll speak first.

The MAYOR leaves the office, followed by BACKSCRATCHER. He separates the COM-MUNITY and the POLICEMAN, and begins talking to the Puerto Ricans.

MAYOR
Now everyone, calm down and listen to me. I feel this deeply in my heart and...
The COMMUNITY reacts simultaneously with anger.

MAYOR
...what happened here in Branch Brook Park is a very serious matter. Now we have to

calm down in order to resolve the incident.

When the MAYOR sees the COMMUNITY is not responding, he calls BACKSCRATCH-ER so that he speaks to them.

BACKSCRATCHER
Please, please! Calm down! We have to listen to what the Mayor is trying to say. He represents authority for this city. We will never be able to resolve this issue if we don't do things properly...

The COMMUNITY keeps yelling (in Spanish and English) at BACKSCRATCHER with the same anger. They do not trust his ulterior motive. The MAYOR interrupts BACKSCRATCHER.

MAYOR *scared*
What are they saying?

BACKSCRATCHER
They're saying that they are tired of being pushed around and being lied to; that this time they want action and that we don't represent them...

MAYOR
I'm very sorry but I can't waste my time with you. You have got to organize and select representatives. I'll meet with those representatives on Monday, a working day.

The MAYOR exits, leaving BACKSCRATCHER with the community. He talks to them, trying to gain their trust. They all leave, little by little, gathering in groups to discuss the issue without him.

BACKSCRATCHER
I can represent this community because I have a lot of experience in these matters. I was Special Assistant to 453 programs against poverty. I managed to get them to build those projects on Seventh Avenue. I've been working for this community for thirty years. There is no one in this community better prepared for this than me. I know more English than any of you...

Only AURORA TROUBLEMAKER is still there listening to him.

BACKSCRATCHER
...and they know me at the Mayor's office. I'm not doing this for myself; I do it for my people, who I hold in the most esteem.

BACKSCRATCHER begins to sing "La Borinqueña." AURORA TROUBLEMAKER joins in.

BACKSCRATCHER
La tierra de Borinquen,
Donde he nacido yo,
Es un jardín florido
De mágico primor...

They continue to sing as they walk and exit the stage. The COMMUNITY gets together on the opposite side of the stage to plan their strategy.

SCENE 4.
A community meeting, at any given place.

NEIGHBOR 1
This is not the first time something like this happens.

NEIGHBOR 2
Police have been aggravating us for a long time already, when they're supposed to be there to protect the people.

NEIGHBOR 3
We need more Puerto Ricans in the Police Department.

NEIGHBOR 4
That won't help because in order to work with them you have to be like them.

NEIGHBOR 5
They killed two members of our community. When is this going to stop?

NEIGHBOR 6
When we make them listen. We've kept quiet for too long.

NEIGHBOR 7
We never complain. That's why things are the way they are.

NEIGHBOR 8
They know they arrested a couple of people who were injured.

NEIGHBOR 1
Yes, and they ran over a woman and her child, on a horse.

NEIGHBOR 2
They don't want to listen to us because we are not organized.

NEIGHBOR 3
Then, let's organize.

NEIGHBOR 4
We have to choose representatives.

NEIGHBOR 5
Yes, but we can't let opportunists like Backscratcher to come and represent us, because they'll want whatever benefits them, not us.

NEIGHBOR 6
Then, let's choose our own representatives, from the community.

NEIGHBOR 7
Yes, let's put together our own committee.

NEIGHBOR 8
And call it *The People's Committee.*

They pick up their banners expressing the demands of the community to go form a picket line in front of City Hall and present them to the Mayor.

SCENE 5.

At the Mayor's office, and in front of City Hall. The COMMUNITY is picketing in front of City Hall. Every now and then, the MAYOR looks at the protesters from his window. BACKSCRATCHER and AURORA TROUBLEMAKER walk towards the entrance of City Hall. The ARMED POLICEMAN who guards the door stops them by pointing his shotgun at them.

BACKSCRATCHER
I've come to see the Mayor. It's important.

The ARMED POLICEMAN lets him through but stops AURORA TROUBLEMAKER.

BACKSCRATCHER
It's alright, she's with me.

AURORA is let through as well.

BACKSCRATCHER
Good morning, Mr. Mayor, Sir.

MAYOR
Oh, good morning, Joe. Come on in.

BACKSCRATCHER
We have formed a committee to deal with the issue of the Puerto Rican community, rather, the Hispanic community. We call it the Hispanic Emergency Council, and I am the Chairman. I have brought with me Miss Aurora Troublemaker, also a member of the Council.

MAYOR
How do you do? Well, Joe, so you're the Chairman, eh? Very good, very good. Maybe we can work something out together. You know, you scratch my back, and I'll scratch yours.

They both head outside. The MAYOR puts his arm over BACKSCRATCHER's shoulders.

NEIGHBOR 1
Those people do not represent our community! These are the demands of our community! These are our demands!

The demands are written both in Spanish and English. BACKSCRATCHER reads them to the Mayor, translating those in Spanish.

BACKSCRATCHER
-Liberty, amnesty, and free medical treatment for those injured.
-A committee from the community to review the Police Department.
-The firing of the Director of Police.

MAYOR
Oh, no, he's my friend. I can't do that.

BACKSCRATCHER
-That a *People's Committee* be formed to investigate the incident at Branch Brook Park with the Puerto Rican community.

MAYOR
What you are asking is unreasonable. I'll tell you what I'll do. I'll ask the Police Commissioner to investigate these issues and give me a detailed report. Is that all right with you?

NEIGHBORS *in unison*
No!!!

FEMALE NEIGHBOR 1
Mr. Mayor, the Black community of Newark burned the city two or three years ago because they were tired of protesting and not being heard! Are you on your people's side or not?

MAYOR *indignant*
I want to make one thing perfectly clear: I am the Mayor.

The COMMUNITY drops their banners and break into a full blown riot, destroying stores and fighting with police throughout Seventh Avenue. They exit the stage through the front, towards the audience.

SCENE 6.
In a factory, in the city center. Two Puerto Rican women discuss the previous events while working on their machines.

FEMALE NEIGHBOR 3
You can't fix things with violence. That never gets you anything.

FEMALE NEIGHBOR 4
Well, the Black community got something. Poor people have no power. We kill ourselves working at factories but we have no voice or vote in the things happening up there. You try the right way but then comes a point when you can't stand it anymore. What happened here in Newark was not planned by anyone in particular. People had been accumulating a lot of anger for a long time, and that anger exploded through violence, because we are human beings, not animals, because we have self-respect, like everybody else, because we want rights that are ours, because we want to be respected.

FEMALE NEIGHBOR 3
But we Puerto Ricans are pacifists. People are going to say we are savages.

FEMALE NEIGHBOR 4
That's exactly why we haven't gained some respect, because we accept everything they do to us, without making a sound.

FEMALE NEIGHBOR 3
But really, a bunch of punks are to blame for all that violence at the Park.

FEMALE NEIGHBOR 4
It wasn't a bunch of punks. They were adults, people with children to think of, women, men, old people. Plus, those you call punks are the ones that suffer the most because they're growing up without good schools to go to, because good schools are not made for "pororicans." The school system is racist and says Puerto Ricans are stupid, that we're only good for working at factories, to wash dishes, and be janitors. Those you call 'punks' are our youth and they've lost their faith in the future. Because there is no future in a disgusting ghetto like this one. What's going to happen when those youngsters marry and have kids? They won't find any jobs, or decent neighborhoods to raise their kids in. And that's why our youth is taking to the streets. Because, in the end, they see no other way to express themselves than through violence.

FEMALE NEIGHBOR 3
Yes, but destroying our supermarkets, our stores, our buildings...

FEMALE NEIGHBOR 4
Those things are not ours. Those stores and buildings belong to rich owners who come here to make money by day, and run like the devil towards the suburbs by night, because they fear the Blacks and Puerto Ricans in Newark. How many of us have the money to buy a store or a building? What we make only pays for food and rent in the places we live, buildings infested with rats and cockroaches.

We hear a heart-breaking cry coming from the audience. The COMMUNITY returns from within the audience onto the stage and confronts POLICE. They all fall, clubbed down, and pile up on the center of the stage. They slowly begin to recover and get back up to confront the audience, repeating the phrase, "Our community demands."

NEIGHBOR 1
Our community demands liberty, amnesty, and free medical treatment for those injured.

NEIGHBOR 2
Our community demands a committee from the community to review the Police Department.

NEIGHBOR 3
Our community demands the firing of the Director of Police.

NEIGHBOR 4
Our community demands that a *People's Committee* be formed to investigate the incident at Branch Brook Park with the Puerto Rican community.

END OF PLAY

THE LATINO ERA
(1980)

Co-written with Dolores Prida.

A comedy with music in one act.

CHARACTERS

MANNY	WOMAN
CHAGO	YOUNG WOMAN
MUSICIANS (congas, piano, bass)	MAN
	YOUNG MAN

The action takes place at CHAGO's apartment in El Barrio, and in his imagination. Thus, there are two areas which blend at times. One of them is CHAGO's actual working space: a table, a typewriter, books, paper, telephone, and a trunk from which the props for the parade scene will be taken out. The other area is where four characters and the MUSICIANS wait sometimes impatiently to be activated by CHAGO, the playwright. The characters sit side by side on four chairs. Close by them the MUSICIANS sit by their instruments; there is interaction between them and the characters. At times, CHAGO finds the characters take over the action. Although sometimes the characters perform MANNY's ideas, it is done through CHAGO's willingness to work them out. There are no props except in the parade scene. Characters should not be dressed alike, but with costumes that lend themselves to the different roles they play. The exchang of ideas occur between MANNY and CHAGO, or CHAGO and his characters; never between MANNY and the characters.

In the darkness, we can hear the sound of the typewriter. Gradual light reveals a kitchen. Mother and daughter are sitting at the table. There is tension between them. The daughter hesitates before speaking.

YOUNG WOMAN
Mum *(Typing ceases)*, I have something to tell you. And I don't know how to say it.

WOMAN
I'll cook pork chops tonight... with rice.

YOUNG WOMAN
Mum, listen to me. (*Pause*) I am pregnant.

WOMAN
Better do a soup. Because, didn't I cook pork chops on Monday?

YOUNG WOMAN
Mum, didn't you hear me? I'm expecting.

WOMAN *crying*
Good Lord, how could you do this to me? Who's the bastard? How did it happen?
When? Where?

YOUNG WOMAN
It was Mr. Roberts, *mi jefe*. Three months ago. During coffee break. I don't know how.

WOMAN
Well, he'll marry you. Won't he?

YOUNG WOMAN
He's married... to another woman.

WOMAN
Holy Virgin Mary! (*Crying*) What would people say? (*Hateful*) I won't raise your
child. Don't you bring him here.

YOUNG WOMAN
Don't worry. I'm not going to have the baby. I'm having an abortion.

WOMAN *Crying harder*
You poor thing! An American has dishonored my daughter. Your brother's going to
kill him. Mark my words.

YOUNG MAN
(*Gets up from his chair, approaches women*) Who do I have to kill?

Light over CHAGO, sitting at his typewriter, writing.

CHAGO
The brother comes in, "Who do I have to kill?" No, the brother's not in yet.

YOUNG MAN heads back to his chair.

CHAGO
Let me think... Yes, he comes in.

YOUNG MAN
(*Back with the women*) What's for dinner?

YOUNG WOMAN
Soup.

YOUNG MAN
Soup again? You know I don't like soup. I always hated it. You know it.

WOMAN
(*Out of control*) Ay!

YOUNG MAN
Mum, what's wrong? (*Looks at YOUNG WOMAN*) What's going on here? It was you.
You're always giving her a headache.

WOMAN
It's nothing, son, calm down. Do you want a beer?

CHAGO
Beer? No, better make it coffee.

Woman discards the beer and hands the YOUNG MAN a cup of coffee.

CHAGO
He takes a sip.

YOUNG MAN is going to take a sip.

CHAGO
No, no. He puts the cup down on the table and stares at the women.

YOUNG MAN follows instructions.

YOUNG MAN
Well? (*Waits for his lines*)

CHAGO
And... Well, so what...?

CHAGO is stuck with the dialogue. Gets up from his chair and paces around.

CHAGO
Well, well, there must be...? No, they tell him. No, hmm. He asks. He knows something's wrong.

Characters wait for their lines.

CHAGO
They were both nervous. No, maybe he... I've got it.

Goes back to his chair.

CHAGO
The father comes in.

MAN
(*Getting up from his chair*) What's for dinner?

YOUNG MAN
Soup. (*They look at each other in confusion*)

MAN
You know I don't like soup. We've been married for forty years and you still don't know how I loathe soup.

WOMAN
(*With apprehension, bursting with tears, hands him an avocado*) We're having avocado with it.

MAN
(*Throwing the avocado against a wall*) What do I care about avocados! I don't want soup.

MAN pauses. He looks at each one. The WOMAN cries harder. The actors wait impatiently for their lines. They glance at CHAGO, who looks at them, impotently. There is a knock at the door.

CHAGO *enthusiastically*
Someone knocks the door.

They knock harder. CHAGO looks around startled, More knocks.

MANNY *from the outside.*
Chago, Chago, it's me, Manny. Open up.

CHAGO opens the door. MANNY enters. He's excited, half drunk.

MANNY
We have to celebrate. Let's drink to the good times ahead. The Latino Era is here and we'll be right up front.

CHAGO
What's up with you? What's the deal today?

MANNY
This is it. It's happening. This time we have good connections.

CHAGO
We've been down this road before.

MANNY
We are going to Broadway. Picture the flashing lights reading, "From El Barrio to Broadway."

CHAGO
What the hell are you talking about?

MANNY
About the greatest Latino musical Broadway has ever seen. I'm talking about a Tony, a movie, an Oscar, the book... and lots of money for us. Lots of dough, you know?

CHAGO
I see, another one of your great ideas. Look, I'm busy. I'm writing a serious play.

MANNY tears the paper off the typewriter. CHAGO tries to rescue it.

MANNY
A serious play. What's more serious that making money?

CHAGO *smoothing out the crumpled paper*
Are you crazy? Are you drunk?

MANNY
Yes, I've been drinking, and do you know with who? Take a guess. No, no, don't. You'll never guess.

CHAGO
OK, I won't. With who?

MANNY
With Joseph King.

CHAGO
Joseph *quién*?

MANNY
Not *quién*; King. You don't know who Joe King is? He's the greatest, the most famous and successful producer in New York City, in the United States, in Europe, in the whole wide world. (*He shows CHAGO the card Joe King has given him*)

CHAGO
OK, so you talked to Joseph King. So what?

MANNY
So what? He's interested in producing your play. I was sitting at that bar on 52nd street, *Frankie & Johnnie*. I started talking to this guy about shows and things like that when he says he's Joseph King. And I said, "I know who Joseph King is." We talked a bit more and I told him, "I'm also involved in the show business. You know what I'd like to see? A Latino musical on Broadway." And Joseph King says to me, "I've also thought about that. I think the time has come to present a Latino musical on Broadway. I've been looking for a good property, but haven't found anything I like." And right then a light went on in my head and I said to him, "Joe, baby, look no further. I have that play." And I told him about this extraordinary script I have. He was very interested and said to get it to him early tomorrow. Tomorrow at 9:00am I will be in his office with the script.

CHAGO
What script?

MANNY
Your script. The one you'll be writing tonight. We have to write it, revise it, and...

CHAGO
But, what script?

MANNY
What script?! (*Long pause*) The script of a play that presents us in such a way that Americans understand us. A play that is Latino but American at the same time, like Mom's mango pie. A play that people from Westchester, Union City, California, Miami, and El Barrio can all understand and have fun with. And pay twenty bucks to see. A play that will announce the coming of the Latino Era. A play that, full of joy, will get the message out: our time has come. (*Pause*) That's the play.

CHAGO
And you want to write that play in a day?

MANNY *checks his watch*
In a night. In twelve hours.

CHAGO
Are you crazy? I've just spent two weeks trying to write a scene. Two weeks for a single scene! Plus, that's not my thing. Broadway is all fake; I write about reality, flesh and blood, about what we see out there. You know what's out there? Drugs, crime, unemployment, buildings with no heating, long lines at the welfare office, people starving, or in gangs, our young people in and out of prisons like revolving doors. (*Pause*) That's what I write about: single mothers, factory workers, mothers raising their children on soup, on stamps. Plus, that thing about the Latino Era being here is bullshit.

MANNY
Yes, I know that there are those problems out there, but there's more. There are people's dreams. One can dream on the welfare line. Young people in prison dream of freedom. Factory workers dream of a better life. Those unwed mothers want to sing and dance. The streets of El Barrio are not beautiful, but they are full of beautiful people doing beautiful things. People are tired of hearing about their own misery. Americans are tired of being blamed for our problems. We have to tell our story in a different way. We have to clean up our act.

CHAGO
I have no interest in writing for those people. I want to write for my own, my people, real people in El Barrio.

MANNY
Real people from El Barrio don't want to hear more sad stories. They work everyday.

On weekends they want to forget their problems; they want to have fun, even if it's for a couple of hours. Why go on and on about their misery? They know misery, alright. They want to see funny people doing funny things, laughing. You know what's out there? Our young people carrying Sony music boxes, salsa music coming out of every window, people leaving work to go see Iris Chacón and Olga Briski. But you don't want to see that. You are locked up in this depressing hole writing tragedies that no one wants to see. We are a good team, Chago. Trust me. You have to think big. With pizzazz, razzmatazz, and all that jazz. Give us a break, man. Give yourself a break. This is the big break.

BROADWAY MELODY OF 1980 (Song I)

MANNY: Broadway, Broadway, here we come.
              Open wide, we're coming in.
              It's our era, it's our time,
              Time for us to do our thing.
              Conga, salsa, put that in,
              That and more. Let's think big.
              Curtain up, light the lights,
              It's our turn, the show begins.

CHORUS: Something's coming, something good.
              Don't cry for me, Loisaida,
              For everything is coming up roses
              In Camelot.
              Mañana, mañana, follow the yellow brick road
              And let's dream the impossible dream
              In Camelot.
              Broadway, Broadway, here we come.
              I think we've got it.
              By Jorge, we've got it.
              The garbage in the Bronx stays on the streets
              For everything is coming up roses
              In Camelot.
              Oh, what a beautiful evening, oh, what a beautiful night.
              I have the funniest feeling
              That everything is coming up roses
              In Camelot.

ALL: Broadway, Broadway, here we come.
                        Open wide, we're coming in.
                        It's our era, it's our time,
                        Time for us to do our thing.
                        Conga, salsa, put that in,
                        That and more. Let's think big.
                        Curtain up, light the lights,
                        It's our turn, the show begins.

                        (Repeat)

WOMAN
God, what a hodgepodge!

MAN
You have to be more original. That's not Latin music.

YOUNG WOMAN
I liked it. Broadway, Broadway... la, la, la...

YOUNG MAN
But that has nothing to do with me.

CHAGO
Manny, it's not as easy as you think.

MANNY *places a new sheet of paper in the typewriter*
You don't know until you try it. My motto is: you have to try everything at least once.
Write.

CHAGO
I can't. And in twelve hours. (*Pause*) Wait a second. This has to be about our experiences. ...A second. Let me think.

YOUNG MAN
Wait a minute. Something is missing. ...A minute. I get ideas but they won't come out.
I get stuck... A true story.

YOUNG MAN and CHAGO
...A second. Hold it. I've got it. I've got it.

YOUNG MAN

The story of my life. It's the night of the blackout. Everybody hits the streets to take advantage of the darkness.

WOMAN

I'll take these diapers. I'll stuck up for a couple of weeks since they're so expensive.

MAN

I need new clothes. This fits me well. I can sell the rest at a bargain.

YOUNG WOMAN

Angel, Angel, get out of there. The cops are shooting at anyone they find in the stores. Run, run.

YOUNG MAN carries off a TV set. He arrives at home.

MAN

Son, we were in real need of a TV but, is it stolen? I've taught you to earn things by the sweat of your brow. I don't want my son to be a thief.

YOUNG MAN

But, Dad, everybody is taking things from the stores. You always wanted a TV set. This is our chance. The owners are insured. Everybody's doing it.

MAN

In that case, my son, there's a difference between being honest and being stupid. This set is black and white. Why didn't you get a color one?

YOUNG MAN

Damn it, you're right. I'll exchange it for a color set. (*Goes back to the store. Stops. Addresses the audience*) I went back and the cops nabbed me. I don't want to go back in there for anything in the world.

MANNY *interrupts*

This can't be, man. Not with our reputation. We're known as disorderly and thieves. We can't present this. How about the people who did not loot during the blackout? Let's take it from the top. It's the night of the blackout. There's a group of Latinos having dinner at *Tavern of the Green*. Lights go out. Everybody panics, but not the Latinos. They remain cool, calm, and collected. Each one takes a candle, gets up, and joins a conga line that snakes among the tables. Little by little, everyone joins. They go out of the restaurant dancing into the night in Central Park.

WOMAN *dropping her candle*
And how many Latinos have you seen having dinner at *Tavern of the Green*?

MANNY *to CHAGO*
You have to use your imagination.

CHAGO
Look, if this is how it's going to go, you write it.

MANNY
You're the writer. You write it. You have talent, but you have to think positive. You have to bring out the extraordinary.

CHAGO
What do I care about extraordinary! Extraordinary, my ass. This is ridiculous. I don't want to ridicule my characters.

MANNY
Your characters are whatever you want. But you can't rush it. Take it easy. Take it slow. One thing at a time. An ounce of patience... you know the rest. Let's try something else. For example, we could have a little number here: fast, funny, sexy, featuring a beautiful chick who can sing, dance, and act the whole package.

YOUNG WOMAN
I get you. What you see here is the next Rita Moreno plus. Make way!

BROADWAY BUMP AND GRIND (Song II)

I want my name on the door
Of a fancy dressing room
Flashing lights around my mirror
And my body well adorned
By an agent, and a contract
And upmarket, swanky clothes.

I'll be making quite an entrance
Fans and flowers galore

Bravo, bravo, viva, viva
At the sight of my appearance
Limo at the theater's door
In the spotlight, I'm the diva
Close-up of my Latin hips
Naked shoulders, oh, zoom in.

I want my name on the covers
Of the beauty magazines
High up twinkling in Times Square
Find my picture everywhere
Get a Tony, and an Emmy
Be an Oscar nominee.

I'll thank my friends in El Barrio
And at the drama workshop
This prize is for everybody
But I think I'll keep it now.
But I think I'll keep it now.
But I think I'll keep it now.
But I think I'll keep it now.

MANNY
That's it. Something like that.

CHAGO *sarcastically*
Are you kidding? Did you take that seriously? It was a joke, man. I'd never put that in
a play of mine. No, that doesn't work.

MANNY
Let's find something that works.

CHAGO
Manny, it's not that easy.

MANNY
Relax, we'll get there.

CHAGO
I can't. My head...

MANNY
Don't give up so easily, man. We can do it. You do your part, I'll do mine. (*Pause*) What
you need is a cup of coffee. (*He goes to prepare the coffee*)

CHAGO *typing*
Mum: "I'll make pork chops tonight." (*He studies what he just wrote*) No.

MANNY is back with the coffee

CHAGO
It won't come out. My head's stuck on the scene I was working on when you got here.

CHAGO takes a sip of his coffee. He has a sudden burst of creativity.

CHAGO
There, it's coming. (*Types*)

MANNY
Good. Finally.

*YOUNG MAN is getting ready to shoot heroin in the kitchen. WOMAN, his mother,
paces and observes him.*

WOMAN
My Lord, what have I done to deserve this? Didn't I sacrifice enough, working day
and night for these scamps? Didn't I go to church every Sunday and lit candles for the
saints? Why is this happening to me?

YOUNG MAN
Ma, give me the matches.

WOMAN *dries a tear, gives him matches*
I tried, but what can a mother do in a neighborhood like this? I'm a single mother. It's
hard to raise boys. (*Praying in front of Saint Jude*) My dear St. Jude, patron of impossible causes, if I went to the psychic it wasn't because I doubted your power. It was just
in case. I can't do this anymore. This son of a gun won't give me a rest. He just came out
of prison and look at him, going at it again. (*To her son*) Why did you come back here?

The YOUNG MAN has injected himself. Falls on floor with an overdose.

WOMAN
I didn't mean that. You are my son, the cross I bear. (*She embraces him*) God, help me. (*Frantically*) I believe in one God, the Father Almighty, maker of Heaven and... (*Out of character*) God, no. We can't present a scene like this.

YOUNG MAN *gets up*
This drug scene is boring. Why don't you write about the pushers. Maybe you can sell it as a *Kojac* episode.

WOMAN
Someone must be financing this operation.

YOUNG MAN
Sure, it's a business.

WOMAN
It may be that even police is behind all this.

CHAGO
Right. We have to write about that too. We can't portray ourselves as junkies by nature.

MANNY
Enough of this drug and drama stuff. That's not how it goes. The majority of Latino families don't have drug problems. Let's change that scene a little bit. There is the mother...

CHAGO *typing*
The mother...

MANNY
The father...

CHAGO *typing*
The father...

MANNY
The son...

CHAGO *typing*
The son... and the Holy Spirit.

MANNY
The son is a Puerto Rican who's going to Harvard University...

YOUNG MAN
Dad, mum, my letter from Harvard arrived. I have been accepted by Columbia and Yale, too, but I prefer Harvard. That's were the best brains of the country get bigger. I'll study molecular biology. I'll dedicate myself to cancer research.

The father is deadly ill, sitting by the mother.

MAN
Thanks, my son. I'm grateful for that, but it's too late for me.

YOUNG MAN
No, dad. I'll save you, and others, regardless of race, sex, religion, national origin, and lifestyle. Someday, I'll win the Nobel Prize. It's a matter of effort. And I'm ready and willing to take this on.

MAN *weak a voice*
Our efforts will not be in vain.

CHAGO *typing*
I'll send my blessing from the grave.

MAN
...from the grave.

MANNY
Here we go again. No graves. You're getting morbid again. Start from, "I am ready and willing..." Cross out the grave.

CHAGO's typewriter and CHARACTERS
Clack, clack, clack, clack, clack

YOUNG MAN
I'm ready and willing...

CHAGO *typing*
...to take this on.

MANNY
Now he sings a song: "Mom and Dad, you've made me a winner."

MUSICIANS play some chords.

MUSICIAN I
Yeah, it's about time for some music.

YOUNG MAN *sings*

No germ will stand in my way
I am ready and willing to fight
Mom and Dad, I will triumph some day.

MANNY
Then he dances trying to cheer up his parents.

YOUNG MAN dances tap.

MANNY
Then he goes to study.

CHAGO *typing*
He goes to study...

MANNY
He graduates summa cum laude.

CHAGO *typing*
He graduates.

MANNY
He does research at the Rockefeller Institute.

CHAGO *typing*
He does research...

MANNY
He discovers a cure for cancer.

CHAGO *typing*
...a cure for cancer.

MANNY
He receives a letter from Sweden.

CHAGO *typing*
...a letter from Sweden.

WOMAN *reading the letter*
"Dear Mr. Pérez, It is with great pleasure that the Nobel Prize Committee would like to inform you that...

MANNY
Hold it. She should sing.

MUSICIAN II
Well, if you ask me, this is a perfect spot for an aria. (*Plays*)

WOMAN *singing*
...you have been chosen as our laureate in Medicine for your astonishing discoveries in your arduous fight against cancer.

MUSICIANS and other CHARACTERS singing
Against cancer.

YOUNG MAN
Mum, dad, I've won the Noble Prize. I've discovered a cure for cancer!

YOUNG MAN takes out a flask, offers spoonful to father, who gets cured immediately. All stand triumphatly and smiling.

MANNY
Now they sing another song: a song of hope and triumph.

CHORUS *sings*
Against cancer.

CHAGO
No one's going to buy this. This scene is going nowhere.

MANNY
Maybe if we take the song out... No, no, I guess you're right. We over did it. Let's go

in a different direction.

CHAGO
Hey, Manny, you know what we haven't tried yet? The most important thing, man: romance, love...

MANNY
No sex. We can't put in any sex in the first Latino play on Broadway. It makes Americans uncomfortable. But romance is not a bad idea. How about something dealing with Latin lovers, you know, the passionate man, the supermacho type. That may work. I can help you with this scene. I have a lot of experience in that area, he, he, he.

CHAGO
Well, let me see... (*Types*) There are Pedro and Tina. They've met that night. They dance at the *Chateau Madrid.*

MANNY
Make that a discotheque, like *Xenon.*

YOUNG MAN
From the moment I first met you, my heart throbbed full of new feelings. I don't know if it was your eyes or your lips or that I was impatient because of the long wait. What a beautiful dawn, to see the sunrise with you. Love me, sweetheart, because I will always adore you. Those big, round... pearls you keep save in your red velvet provoke me. Sweetie, I crave you with a passion. I want to kiss them... and you. I'm so in love. I want you to be mine. I can't stand the thought of living without you. Marry me.

YOUNG WOMAN
I'm not ready. I don't know how to sew, nor broom. And I can only cook soup.

YOUNG MAN
Soup! My favorite dish... and made by your ivory hands. I would eat soup every day of my life just to be with you.

YOUNG WOMAN
In that case, what are we waiting for?

MUSICIANS *play the wedding march*
Forty years later...

MAN
What's for dinner?

WOMAN
Soup.

MAN
Soup again. We've been married for forty years. Forty years of soup. What a life.

WOMAN *crying*
When we started dating, you used to love soup.

MAN *throws pot out*
Yeah, but now we are married.

MANNY
Chago, what's the matter with you? You are always stuck in the same scene. Change, man.

CHAGO
What's wrong with that scene?

MANNY
Everything. That's not a love scene. It has to be more romantic, like us. We Latinos are very romantic. And romance can be universal. Everybody can identify with that. (*Pause*) Something's coming... Type: Her name is María. His name is Tony. She is Puerto Rican. A lovely young woman, very innocent. He...

YOUNG MAN *singing*
María, I just met a girl named María.

YOUNG WOMAN *singing*
Tony, Tony...

MAN *interferes between them. YOUNG MAN kills him.*

YOUNG MAN *singing*
There's gonna be a rumble tonight...

WOMAN *singing*
A boy like that, who killed your brother...

CHAGO
Hey, Manny, that sounds familiar.

MANNY
Yes, it's been done before, but maybe we can change a few things. Go on.

CHAGO
María is crying in the kitchen. Anita comes in and says, "I'm going to cook pork chops tonight."

MANNY
Your pork chops are coming out of my ears. Something is wrong with you, Chago. These pork chops and soup keep popping up everywhere. Did you have a starving childhood?

CHAGO
Pork chops are my favorite dish, but we could only afford soup. I remember one day my mother and I were in the kitchen and she said...

MANNY
That's it. I know what's happening, man. All your scenes take place in the kitchen. Let's get out of the goddam kitchen. Let's have a scene out of the house, where we can see Latinos interacting with other people. Check it out, have a think.

CHAGO
A factory... the subway... a long line at the...

YOUNG WOMAN, WOMAN, and MAN line up at the Welfare Office. YOUNG MAN is the interviewer.

WOMAN *pregnant*
Hey, fuck's going on? Line ain't moving. It's ten to five. Been here since the break of dawn and all these people do is waste time. Dude's (THE INTERVIEWER) taken like five coffee breaks already. This kid's gonna pop out if you keep me waiting here like this.

YOUNG MAN *as interviewer*
What's she saying?

YOUNG WOMAN *as prostitute*
She's saying it's ten to five and she's been here all day and she's gonna have her baby here if you don't hurry up and stop taking coffee breaks.

MAN *drunk*
Grab an ashtray and throw it to his face. Coffee break, my ass. He leaves every five

minutes to take a hit.

YOUNG WOMAN *to INTERVIEWER*
Dude, could you hurry up? I gotta go to work. Listen, honey, I gotta get out of here. I gotta take care of business.

WOMAN
Girl, you work during the day?

YOUNG WOMAN
Day and night, sweetheart. This welfare check is not enough. Life's tough out there. I have to work overtime.

MAN *inspecting prostitute*
And how's the merchandise?

YOUNG WOMAN
Don't squeeze the tomatoes if you're not gonna buy, bro.

WOMAN
Goodness gracious me! The bunch of lowlifes you have to put with at the welfare line. (*To INTERVIEWER*) Hey, hurry up there. You've been talking to that one for 'bout half an hour. You don't need to do that much to sign that crappy check. Finish up, goddam it. I have to go put the beans in water.

YOUNG MAN
Office is closed. It's five o'clock.

WOMAN
What do you mean, closed? You will see me today. (*Pushes him down on his chair*) I've been here since the break of dawn.

YOUNG MAN
Sorry.

The WOMAN attacks the INTERVIEWER. Everybody gets in. WOMAN has labor pains.

MANNY
Chago, please, this is the same old shit. That welfare scene is in every Latino play I've seen. Cut it out. If we are going to launch the Latino Era we have to show our best side. Look, take that line. You are the writer, Chago, but I have the experience.

CHAGO

Yeah? How about the great magazine you were planning to publish last year? Nation-wide distribution and all that crap.

MANNY

It's true that didn't work out, but I gained a lot of experience.

CHAGO

And the *café-théâtre* you were going to open two years ago?

MANNY

That was something else. There were complications. Things I wasn't counting on. But the past is the past. This time... this is a new beginning. Listen, how about making that line, a line of Latino executives on the way to Wall Street? Wall Street is where it's at, brother. And from that Wall Street line we can...

CHAGO types.

YOUNG WOMAN

Taxi! 80 Wall Street, please. And hurry. I have a very important meeting. I must be punctual. No more Latin time in the corporate world. Do you know what Latin time is?

YOUNG MAN *as taxi driver*

A new dance?

YOUNG WOMAN

No, it's not a dance. It is being at least one hour late. But as for me, well, I didn't get my company, *Tostones, Inc.*, off the ground by being an hour late. Right here. (*She pays and exits the cab.*) Keep the change.

MAN *hailing another cab*

Taxi! 80 Wall Street, please. And hurry. I have a very important meeting. *Tostones, Inc.* is going public. We are going to diversify, too. Soon you will see barbecue *tostones*, onion and garlic *tostones*, cheese *tostones*...

YOUNG MAN

How about sour cream *tostones*?

MAN

That's a great idea! (*Jots it down.*) We can corner the Jewish market, too. I can see it: sour cream *tostones* for Passover. Things are really looking up! I didn't have it this good all the time. I remember, back in El Barrio, when I used to play with fire hydrants...

CHAGO *typing*
And needles...

MANNY
No, take the needles out. We are doing OK so far. Let's follow through. It needs build up. Now they are at a meeting: *Tostones, Inc.*, Board of Directors meeting.

MAN
We are now in the position to get hold of the raw material for our product.

YOUNG MAN
This is the time to acquire the majority of stock in the United Fruit Company. It will finally be owned by Latinos.

WOMAN
Point of order. We should discuss diversification first.

YOUNG MAN
Point of information. There is a motion on the table and I call the question. Anyone seconds this motion?

MAN
That's the second item on the agenda.

YOUNG WOMAN
Dear Sir, diversification is closely linked to the acquisition of the raw material. Let's refer to the charts. Figures don't lie.

WOMAN
But according to our marketing research, the key to our success is in the packaging.

YOUNG MAN
I have a report on the advertising campaign for the new line.

YOUNG WOMAN
I think we should change the name of our product. You think people in Peoria will know what *tostones* are? Why do you think *platanutres* made it in the American market? Because they renamed them *banana chips*! That's why.

MAN
What would you call them? *Banana rounds?*

WOMAN
If we put a hole in the middle we could call them *banadonuts.*

YOUNG MAN
How about putting two *tostones* together with *chili con carne* in the middle and calling them *banawich?*

YOUNG WOMAN
We should go back to the original name: *plátanos.*

MAN
The right word is *guineo.*

WOMAN
It is banana. That's the universal name. Even in Russia they know what a banana is.

YOUNG MAN
Whatever name we choose, what matters is the advertising. *Tostones* will become a household word.

MUSICIANS
You need a jingle, man. Something like:

> Check it out, America
> Fried bananas will get you
> In the mood
> Fried bananas in the morning
> Fried bananas in the afternoon
> And you thought
> They were only cornflakes!

WOMAN
No, no. That's confusing. We are talking about big, green bananas. There are bananas and there are plantains.

MAN
There's *mofongo*, too. We can call it *banamatzo* balls.

YOUNG MAN
Mofongo in the convenient boiling pouch.

YOUNG WOMAN
We are not talking about bananas. We are talking about dollars!

MANNY *interrupting*
Chago, I think you got stuck again. Your English doesn't sound quite right. We have to work on the language. It has to be more idiomatic. It has to flow.

CHAGO
I never write in English.

MANNY
You write, I'll translate. Remember, the public who's going to see this show doesn't understand Spanish. Plus, the Latinos that go to Broadway speak English anyway. But we can throw in some Spanish words that everybody understands, like *sombrero, qué pasa, mira, lo que será, será...* you know, for flavor. We'll kill two *pájaros* with one *piedra*.

CHAGO
We should aim for some sort of universal language. To say things in a way everyone understands.

MUSICIAN 1 *plays some bars*
Music, dude! I've been trying to tell you. This language everybody understands.

MUSICIAN 2 *playing*
You talk too much. Words, words. I'm ready to go to sleep.

YOUNG MAN
Yeah, music and dance. I can say things with my body, too. You can get many messages across through dance.

YOUNG MAN dances. Other characters form a chorus line. The music and dance are Latin.

MANNY
That dance is fine, Chago. I guess we could put in a little dance number like that, but it has to be more sophisticated. You know, maybe a little tap here, a little soft shoe there, a high kick up there...

CHAGO

Yes, we can't say it all with a dance here and a song there.

MUSICIANS react.

MANNY

Sure, the lighting, the costumes, the sets. All of that adds up.

CHAGO

But in real life people don't go about singing and dancing like that. People talk, use words. And in this play we have to deal with some serious stuff too.

MANNY

But, not too serious. People get restless.

CHAGO

Look, Manny, there are things you can't say through music. For example, I saw this picture on the newspaper...

WOMAN

It was the photo of a marine dragging an old lady across the beach. In Vieques. (*Pauses*) Who is this woman? She's near the water. There are people around her. Over there, in the water, one can see dozens of fishing boats full of people. They all carry signs that read, "US Navy Out of Vieques." But the woman is on the beach. She's not carrying a sign but she's talking. In the beginning, we can't hear what she's saying because the wind carries her voice in the other direction. We switch sides. Now we can listen to her voice, worn-out yet firm. (*Pauses*) "I was born on this island and have never left. And never will. My father was a fisherman. So were my husband and my son. Forty years ago they came here with their ships, and bombs, and planes. Made a deal with whoever was in power then. They've pushed us to the side, cornered us like animals. They've kept our best land, our beaches, our waters. They started to store live bombs, put up wired fences, get their ships ashore and start running, to practice their wars here. From land to sea. The nets began to fill up with dead fish. The reefs were blown to pieces. The birds flew away in fear. And the noise –BOOM, BOOM, BOOM– does not stop. The kids sometimes play with live bombs they find buried in the sand. No, I'm not leaving. I am not your enemy. I just want peace on my land. Get out of here. Get your ships and your bombs out of our waters. There won't be any peace until you leave. Quiet. I want a bit of quiet!

MANNY

Too many politics. Too direct. It will never work on Broadway. It is too heavy. Look, that subject is for another type of audience. Maybe Off-Broadway, Off-Off-Broadway. The Vieques issue is very valid. The Navy having their target-practice on that island, destroying the ecology, the fishermen's livelihood. Bombing the hell out of that island, killing all that fish –but not for this play. We would close after an opening night. We are going to Broadway. You have to keep the audience in mind. See, we have to put in our flavor, our culture, because that's what Broadway audiences want to see, traditional stuff.

CHAGO
If what you want is *Chiquita Banana* kind of characters, I'm sorry for you, buddy, that's not my thing. Plus, I respect Latino actors too much to write such things.

MANNY
What are you talking about? What do you think that scene with the blackout was? Let me tell you: pure, unaltered stereotype!

CHAGO
Tsk. But that's different. Do you know what happens when Latino actors go to auditions?

YOUNG WOMAN
"We need a Puerto Rican for this part, but you don't look Puerto Rican enough."

MAN
"You look too Hispanic. And in this play there are no gangs and no drug addicts. Don't call us, we'll call you."

WOMAN
"I think you would be good for the part of the prostitute. (*Pauses*) Or the maid."

MANNY
You, the writers, are to blame. You're the ones coming up with those roles.

CHAGO
If they don't write stereotypes, those writers won't sell their script.

MANNY
Why don't you do something about it? You're a writer, aren't you? Write something different.

YOUNG MAN
Yeah, man. I'd like to play different roles. Hamlet, a doctor, or... a regular person.

YOUNG WOMAN
When they have a play on Broadway with Latino characters, we don't even get those parts.

WOMAN
But if they are stereotypes, why do you want to play those roles anyway?

MAN
Because those plays pay a full salary –they pay union scale. And we actors want to earn a living acting.

YOUNG WOMAN
Now, we must admit that many Latinos have been on Broadway: José Ferrer, Chita Rivera, Raúl Juliá, Rita Moreno, Priscilla López...

WOMAN
And... who else? They are the exception.

YOUNG WOMAN
Why can't we all be exceptional?

MANNY
But we can. We can. See, if we take everything we have and put it in a context of dynamic optimism, then we can go somewhere with this idea. We have to put in a little bit of everything. After all, all Latinos are the same...

CHAGO
Are they?

THE MELTING POT DUET

MANNY: Mexicans, Argentines
                Cubans and Dominicans
                We all came here looking
                For the streets of gold

CHAGO: To get a job

MANNY: We've left our mark on the city

CHAGO: The mark of Zorro

MANNY: Our language, our food, our music

CHAGO: Our skin

MANNY: Give them a play that tells
                All about us, who we are
                We are not primitive people
                We have our culture
                Our history, out thing

CHAGO: Our serious problems

MANNY: Show them our mixture
                Of White, Black, and Indian
                The *charros*, the *gauchos*, the *jíbaros*
                Our cowboys and peasants
                Give them a play like a rainbow
                Serve them a pot of *sancocho*
                Mix in the rhythms, shake in the energy
                Stir in the colors. Package it right!
                That's what will sell
                That's how we'll be
                A box office hit!

While MANNY sings, in response to the lines of the song, CHAGO jokingly, and in conspiracy with the characters, dresses them up: he puts a Mexican hat on the MAN; make up on the YOUNG WOMAN, now a baton twirler; a tie, a suit, and a pava (Puerto Rican straw hat) on the YOUNG MAN, now a politician; sunglasses on the WOMAN, now a TV announcer.

YOUNG WOMAN *excited*
I always wanted to do a Brazilian extravaganza!

CHAGO *typing*
The action takes place during the Columbus Day Parade, along Fifth Avenue.

As WOMAN narrates, the characters also become a gaucho dancer, marching midwives, Queen Isabella and Christopher Columbus. The musicians will play parade music, throw confetti, and parade around as spectators.

WOMAN *as TV presenter, holding a mike and speaking in an Argentinian accent to an invisible TV camera somewhere in the audience*
Good afternoon, dear audience. Here from Fifth Avenue, Rosita Paraguay for Channel 45, your Hispanic TV station. Bringing you all the happiness and splendor of the Columbus Day Parade. The parade begins. A contingent of three hundred *charros* and their horses approaches –three hundred *charros* on horseback! With their lassos and very colorful *sombreros*. They've come from San Antonio, Texas to be with us in the Big Apple for this wonderful event. (*The* charro *gets closer. The TV presenter offers him the mike.*) Hello, is there anything you'd like to say to our audience?

MAN *as* charro
Last year, forty Mexicans were murdered by the border patrol while trying to cross the Rio Grande: José Campos Torres, Ricardo Morales, Ernesto González, Jacinto López (Charro *continues to give names.*)

WOMAN *takes mike away from* charro *trying to change the subject*
It's such a beautiful day today! Nature has been generous with us this afternoon. We are lucky to have such marvelous weather. And such a lovely show! Now we see approaching another beautiful contingent, the Bayamón Baton Twirlers, known the world over. Let's talk for a bit to the main majorette. Let's ask about her horoscope. Miss...

YOUNG WOMAN *as baton twirler*
The annual income of Puerto Ricans in the U.S. is the lowest in the nation. Our housing conditions are the worst. The government is closing hospitals in our neighborhoods...

WOMAN *withdraws microphone quickly*
The parade goes on, dear viewers. Now we see approaching a group of five hundred midwives from the South Bronx. Suitcases in hand, they are ready to bring more Latinos into this world, who will soon be the largest minority. Oh, but what am I looking at, dear viewers? We are proud to have among us this afternoon the very best people of our community, so many of our leaders are with us today. Here's Mr. Starbuck, a politician who's always been so concerned about our community. Sir...

YOUNG MAN *in a strong American accent*
I am delighted to march in this parade with my *amigos*, who I love so *mucho*. I'd like to remind my *amigos* that voting in the coming elections is the right and duty of every citizen. My name is Roberto Starbuck. Remember: *esse-teh-ah-erreh-beh-ooh-ceh-kah*, Starbuck. *Adiós, muchachos!* (*Throws kisses.*)

WOMAN
So nice, isn't he? Oh, here come the beautiful floats! We now see the impressive float

that won the first prize. It's sponsored by that beer you have when you're having one too many. As you can see, it's built in the shape of a ship, of a caravel, and atop travels Queen Isabella of Castile. At her foot on bended knee, we can see admiral Christopher Columbus. They are both surrounded by beautiful *jibaritas* wearing their typical *pavas*, and serapes underneath plantain leaves. Around them, a group of *gauchos* dance the *malambo*. A herd of llamas, and on their backs, twenty-five *rumba* dancers with their *maracas*. Such happiness! So colorful! We see all of our race has gathered here today. Long live Latinos united! (*A street-sweeper begins to sweep the confetti and the TV announcer along with it.*) Dear viewers, this is Rosita Paraguay from Fifth Avenue, saying, (*Throws a kiss as she is swept away*) ciao!

The street-sweeper sweeps her off stage. The band plays, the charro *recites names, the baton twirler gives statistics, the politician spells his name. Total pandemonium.*

CHAGO *screaming*
Stop! I can't do it! We want to say too many things at once. (*He throws himself on the typewriter.*) I am tired. We have been here all night and this is not happening.

MANNY
Yes it is. It's all coming. Don't quit now. I know we are trying to say too much, but let's go on. We are on the right track now.

CHAGO
I can't... I can't... (*He pulls his hair, walks around, and pounds the typewriter.*) I am not going to write anymore. I'll pawn the typewriter. I'm going to sell shaved ice on Lexington and 104th street. This is too hard.

CHAGO collapses on his chair. MANNY tries to revive him by massaging him as if he were a boxer.

MANNY
There's not much time left but we can still do it, man. We can't give up now.

CHAGO
This is all wrong, Manny. We don't even know what to say about ourselves. You want me to write this play their way...

MAN
But, what about all the ideas that have been thrown around?

WOMAN
None of them are good.

MAN
Some were!

YOUNG MAN
But they are all jumbled up.

MUSICIAN 1
There wasn't enough music!

WOMAN
There was too much.

MAN
It should have been all in Spanish.

MUSICIAN 2
With more songs, in English.

MAN
There's not enough crisis.

MUSICIAN 3
This is a joke.

YOUNG MAN
Characters have to be more developed.

YOUNG WOMAN
Enough! This is no good, man. This is junk. I will not be a part of another Latino melting pot disaster!

YOUNG MAN
You see, the problem with us is that we always end up fighting, slapping each other around. Let's see, we can do this: music, dancing, drama, comedy, real life, a message... Let's take it from the top.

CHAGO
There is no time.

MAN
There is time.

MANNY
Of course there is. I'll get more time. I'll call Joe. (*He takes a card out of his pocket and dials the number on the phone.*) Hello, with Mr. King, please. Mr. King? I hope I didn't wake you up, sir. Yes, I know it's five o'clock in the morning, but this is important... Manny... Manny Rivera. Remember? We met last night at *Frankie & Johnnie's.* The bar. You gave me your card. It's about the play. The Latino play you wanted for Broadway. Remember now? No, I don't have the wrong number. I have your card right here. You told me to bring the script over to you by nine o'clock. But, look, Mr. King, I am going to need a little more time. Something's come up... (*Joe King has hung up. MANNY is left speechless.*)

CHAGO
What'd he say?

MANNY
We have all the time in the world.

CHAGO
Hey, hey, hey! Great! We have more time. Then, let's keep working.

MANNY
We have all the time in the world. The whole thing is off. Forget about it. That old drunk didn't even remember me.

WOMAN
Ha! Didn't I say? You can't count on the *gringos.*

YOUNG WOMAN
But I want to go to Broadway!

YOUNG MAN
Forget about it. Forget it. I have a better idea. Quick, before I forget...

MUSICIAN 1
Is there music in it?

YOUNG MAN
Yes, there is.

WOMAN
Drama, comedy?

YOUNG WOMAN
Crisis, real life...?

MAN
Yes, we have all the ingredients. All we have to do is mix them right.

MANNY
Chago, forget it. You can go to sleep now. Take a break. Then you can go back to
writing your kitchen soap operas.

CHAGO
No, no. Now I'm all hot with new ideas. All the characters are up in my head, telling
me things.

YOUNG WOMAN
Now's when we're gonna write this play. We're gonna get this play going.

YOUNG MAN
Write, Chago. (*CHAGO puts paper in the typewriter.*) This is the idea: A writer tries
to write a play for Broadway...

CHAGO *repeats*
A writer tries to write a play for Broadway...

WOMAN
That's the idea, a play about this very experience.

YOUNG MAN
Starts like this: It is... this night.

CHAGO *typing*
It is... this night...

MAN
Chago writes...

CHAGO *typing*
Chago writes on the typewriter...

YOUNG WOMAN
Manny enters and says...

CHAGO *typing*
Manny enters and says...

MANNY
But, why do you want to go on?

CHAGO *typing*
Why do you want to go on?

MANNY
We have no money to do this play.

CHAGO *typing*
We have no money to... (*Stops typing midway.*)

MANNY
Where will it go? (*MANNY exits.*)

CHAGO
Where...

YOUNG WOMAN
Where are we going with this?

MAN
Here we are... with this.

WOMAN
Now we are dealing with this.

Music begins. They all sing...

BROADWAY IS JUST ONE STREET

Where are we going with this?
Where are we going with this?
Started out in El Barrio
That's where it all began
Got together, got walking
Through the city we sang
Broadway is just one street
And there's much more to walk

They say, "Make it to Broadway
And you'll show us you're made"
But if you keep on searching
Through the city you sing
You'll find the play that shows you
There's so much more to see
You can't buy us nor sell us
Let's go write down the truth
There's no rest, on the move

We begin once again
Nothing can stop us now
Let's not wait for tomorrow
Or tomorrow will die
Broadway is just one street
And there's much more to walk

We are here, and a-there
In the streets, everywhere
Through the city we sing
We will make it, you'll see
Broadway is just one street
And there's much more to walk

Where are we going with this?
Here we are... with this
Now we are dealing with this
Broadway is just one street
And there's much more to walk

END OF PLAY

FIRST NIGHT OUT:
THE BASIC TRAINING OF A BAG LADY
(1981)

A comedy with musical implications.

CHARACTERS
LEONOR, a woman in her fifties
ANGELA, a woman in her forties
VIRGINIA, a thin woman, ageless
MADELINE, close to forty

ACT I, SCENE I

SETTING

Sidewalk in front of the New World Savings Bank and the Chicken Wonder fast food joint next door. A giant pile of black plastic bags stands menacingly in front of the chicken joint. Some bags have taken over space in front of the bank; others have spilled their content closer to the gutter. The prominent, almost central bank displays the sign: "A new concept in banking." Shining through the window are other signs: "Grand slam gift giveaway," "no charge 5% checking," "30 months savings certificates," "We're in business to help your business," "Interest on interest," and other sorts of enticing signs.

LEONOR, a bag lady, enters dressed in several layers of clothing: sweaters, blankets, nightgowns, coats, scarves; she pushes a mail carrier where she has collected pieces of rope, cans, umbrellas, a broom, kitchen appliances, folding chairs, articles of clothing, a shopping cart, newspapers, curtains, fabrics, signs... Boxes and shopping bags of different sizes, colors, and materials spell out the names of large and highly successful companies. The carrier is a colourful arrangement of textures and shapes. LEONOR proceeds to inspect the garbage bags; she carefully selects the best pieces of chicken she can find; she meticulously picks the dirt off the best rolls and french fries; she places the food in a small bag.

ANGELA enters pushing the supermarket shopping cart that contains her belongings, and approaches LEONOR's carrier. LEONOR springs out from among the bags.

LEONOR
Hands off. What the hell do you think you're doing? That's my stuff.

ANGELA
I didn't see you. But I knew you were around somewhere.

LEONOR
Sure, sure. What were you looking for in there?

ANGELA
Nothing, nothing. I didn't touch your things. I respect other people's property. I'm warning you: don't get on my nerves. I'm not gonna put up with it. I have had it today. No one is gonna push me around, understand? (*Waves a fist at by passers down the block.*) Get off my back, you bastards. You threw me out of the subway. I paid my fare. (*Laughs*) See them run? I'm not scared of them.

LEONOR
You were gone for days. I figured you took off for good.

ANGELA
You thought I was dead, eh? Well, I'm alive. I fell asleep on the subway, that's all. But here I am. Again. (*Notices the bag of chicken.*) What's that?

LEONOR
None of your business. (*Puts the bag away.*) It's spring already, you know? I shouldn't see your face again until next winter.

ANGELA
Spring already? How do you know?

LEONOR
It's in the air.

ANGELA *smells the fetid air*
Phew, it's in the air all right. Jesus, time flies.

LEONOR
You better get going. I've had it with your screams and fights. You give me a headache. I need some peace and quiet.

ANGELA

It's gonna be quiet. I just came to watch the eclipse. It's gonna happen tonight. It only happens once in a hundred years. I don't want to miss it this time. This is the perfect spot to watch it.

LEONOR

Bullshit. It's too dark up there to see anything.

ANGELA

I know what I'm doing. This (*piece of glass*) is an eclipse lens. All I have to do is adjust it to the light.

LEONOR

Take your goddam lens and move out of here.

ANGELA

You know nothing about astronomy. (*Pushes her cart out of the way, closer to the garbage bags.*) The smell of spring is stronger around here. (*Looks at the bags.*) So many of these all over the city.

LEONOR

There's a garbage strike.

ANGELA

Another one? (*Puts her mat out and starts to get settled.*)

LEONOR

Don't get too comfortable.

ANGELA

This is a free country.

LEONOR

I was here first. Why do you always look for trouble?

ANGELA

I don't. I came here to mind my business and watch the eclipse, and here you are. For you, I'm trouble. For me, you're trouble.

END OF SCENE 1

ACT I, SCENE 2

MADELINE has been listening behind the bags. She takes a sip from a bottle in a paper bag, puts the bag away and approaches the other women.

MADELINE
Do you mind if I listen in?

LEONOR *to ANGELA*
Is she with you?

ANGELA
I don't know her.

LEONOR
Keep going. There's no place for you here.

ANGELA
We were here first. (*Searches the sky with the eclipse lens.*)

MADELINE
I'm not staying long. I just want to talk to you for a while.

LEONOR
Go ahead, talk. What do you want to say? Be quick.

MADELINE
Let's talk, about whatever you want. Let's talk about yourselves.

LEONOR
I don't want to talk. I'm thinking.

MADELINE
What are you thinking about?

ANGELA
(*To LEONOR*) Don't say a word. You don't know who she is.
(*To MADELINE*) Who are you, anyway? What do you want?

MADELINE
I just want to know a little about you.

ANGELA
Who? Me?

MADELINE
Both of you.

ANGELA
What for?

MADELINE
I am a freelance writer. I'm working on an article.

ANGELA
Go work somewhere else. It's too crowded here. (*Examines MADELINE more close-ly.*) You don't look like no writer to me.
(*To LEONOR*) I tell you, she's up to no good.

MADELINE
I can prove it. (*Takes out a tape recorder.*) See?

LEONOR
Angela, take it easy.
(*To MADELINE*) Tell me about it.

MADELINE
It's an article about street dwellers.

LEONOR
Oh, yeah.

ANGELA
Street what?

MADELINE
Street people.

LEONOR
Like you.

ANGELA
Leave me out of this.

MADELINE
I will be the first person to write about this subject. People are curious about what's going on out here. If the article gets through, I might be able to get some television interviews.

LEONOR
What do you want to know?

MADELINE
You can talk about anything you want. Just do what you always do. I just want to stick around for a while. I won't interfere. Well, maybe I'll ask a question or two later.

LEONOR
You interview women only?

MADELINE
No, I'm interested in street people in general. But men are more difficult.

ANGELA
That's right. They're a mess. Like Joe, the drummer. He's always trying to lay on top of me. He talks filthy stuff. He says my body is warm. He grabs me and tries to kiss me. I hate that.

LEONOR
What magazine are you writing for?

MADELINE
The *Journal of American Natural History*.

LEONOR
I've seen that magazine around. It's pretty. Lots of pictures, right? It costs about five dollars. It has things about life in other countries and planets and animals in the jungle and the North Pole, right?

MADELINE
Yes, they publish articles on anthropology, sociology and natural history for the common reader.

LEONOR
That's what I said. I've had it in my hands, but I didn't keep it. I don't have time to read. I'm always on the move.

ANGELA
Did you keep the toaster they gave you? Or did you pawn it?

LEONOR
They didn't give me the toaster. I found it. I'm saving it for something important.

ANGELA *to MADELINE*
Did it start yet?

MADELINE
Not yet. I haven't turned on my tape recorder. (*Turns it on.*)

LEONOR *pulling down a vegetable box from the garbage pile*
Sit down, miss. Make yourself at home.

MADELINE
Call me Madeline, please. What's your name?

LEONOR
Leonor Tuesday.

ANGELA
I thought your name was Leonor Winter.

LEONOR
It isn't. Shut up. People know me as Leonor Tuesday.

ANGELA
Hold it. Is that thing on?

MADELINE
Yes.

ANGELA *grabs the recorder*
Who the hell told you I was going to be part of this?

LEONOR
Come on, stop the bullshit. You're always messing things up. Don't be stupid.

ANGELA
Is it running? How do you stop it? Stop it, stop it. I don't want my voice in there. Get out of here with this thing. I want my words back. Everything I said. I don't want this creep here to put my words in her machine. I don't want to remember a bunch of things I forgot. Get out of here! (*She's ready to throw the machine against the sidewalk.*)

LEONOR
Give me that. (*Rescues the machine and returns it to MADELINE.*) Stop interrupting.

ANGELA
You're gonna make me miss the eclipse.

LEONOR
It serves you right. As far as I'm concerned, you can disappear right now.

ANGELA
Is that how you feel about me? I'm leaving right now. I hope you have a good time with your fucking interview. And with your new friend. I hope I never see your face again. (*Gathers her belongings and exits.*)

MADELINE
I'm sorry.

LEONOR
What about?

MADELINE
I didn't mean to upset her.

LEONOR
Some days anything ticks her off.

MADELINE
You must know her well.

LEONOR
Some days I do. She comes and goes. She talks to herself. She lies. I don't pay attention. You better erase all the crap she said.

MADELINE
Oh, no. everything is important. I can use all the information. Every gesture, every word has value. I want to capture the suspense of real life. I learn from everything each one of you says.

END OF SCENE 2

ACT I, SCENE 3

VIRGINIA enters in a neat outfit of collected garments, shopping bags in hand, wiping off her skirt and legs.

VIRGINIA
Shit. It won't come off; it won't come off. They drive like maniacs in this city.

LEONOR
Virginia, I didn't recognize you at first. You look so elegant.

VIRGINIA
What do you mean? I always dress like this. I was taking off today and look what happens.

LEONOR
What?

VIRGINIA
It was a white truck. It sneaked up on me. It creeped up slowly and, shhhhhhh, it sprayed me.

LEONOR *examines her dress*
It's just water. It will dry soon.

VIRGINIA
It's not water. It's something else. I don't know what. It's ruined my dress. I better wash it before it sticks. You have any water? A big white truck. A gorilla was driving it.

LEONOR gives her a plastic water bottle.

VIRGINIA
Is this really spring water?

LEONOR
No, hydrant water. Just the same. It cleans. Good for drinking too. What brings you here? I thought you'd be south by now.

VIRGINIA *wiping her dress*
I was going this afternoon. But now I don't know. I can't get on a bus looking like this. Look at my dress.

LEONOR
It's clean now. It will dry out in no time.

VIRGINIA
Good, 'cause I don't have much time.

LEONOR
What's the big rush? Take it easy. You take things too seriously.

VIRGINIA
I should have left yesterday, the way I planned. This wouldn't have happened.

LEONOR
Relax. You won't last long rushing that way.

VIRGINIA *returning the water bottle*
Who wants to live long?

LEONOR
I do. And my friend Madeline, here. Am I correct, Madeline?

VIRGINIA
I knew something like this was going to happen today. I knew it. I had a dream last night. When I woke up I couldn't remember. That's when I knew something was wrong. I always remember my dreams. This morning I tried and tried, but everything was blank. I knew something bad... Wait a minute. Yes, I remember now. I was going out of the city. I had packed my things and had my ticket ready. When I looked for it I couldn't find it. Someone stole it, I know. I never lose things. It was the last bus out of the city. I missed it.

LEONOR

Forget it. It was only a bad dream. There's hundreds of buses and trains leaving this city every minute of the day, and night.

VIRGINIA

You don't understand. I just have to go. I don't like to make people wait. They're probably at the bus station waiting for me. And I'm not going to be on that bus. Oh, my God. (*Looks in her bags.*) Did the presents get dirty? (*Takes some wrapped items and shows them to LEONOR.*) Yesterday, I spent the whole day shopping. I have presents for everybody. I don't like to go back home with empty hands. My nephew, he's eight, bright young man, he always expects presents, even if he doesn't say it. I don't like to disappoint him. I love that kid. This time I'm bringing him a construction set.

MADELINE

That's nice of you. And that's a pretty dress you're wearing. Did you make it yourself? I wish I could sew like that.

VIRGINIA *gathering her gifts*

Did you hear about the woman they killed in the subway?

LEONOR

That's old news.

VIRGINIA

No, it happened last night.

LEONOR

I didn't read the papers today. I've been busy.

VIRGINIA

They stabbed her ten times. They found her on a bench. The policeman thought she was spending the night.

LEONOR

She probably had money.

VIRGINIA

She had been there for a long time.

LEONOR

Did you see her?

VIRGINIA
There's a photo of her in the paper. Maybe you know her. (*Searches her bag.*)

LEONOR
(*To VIRGINIA*) I don't know her. I'm not interested.
(*To MADELINE*) Virginia sleeps with us in winter. We see her from winter to winter.
She disappears in the summer. I think she goes out of the city.

VIRGINIA
You're damn right. I can't stay in the city all year long. This city is an awful place to
live, a nice place to come back to. I need to see other places; I like traveling, meeting people. But I have to go home, at least once a year. They miss me so much. You
should see the fuss they make over me when I get home: it's always a big celebration.
They want me to stay over there, but I can't now; I'm too independent. I get bored,
you know? I can't be tied down. The first day is all cheers. I tell them everything I've
done during the year (that they should know of). By the second night, I can't stand
it anymore. I have to move on. Besides, I don't want them to get too attached to me
again. Move on, travel, meet people: that's my life. I love the Caribbean. The sea is of
one tone with the sky.

VIRGINIA'S SONG

I've been where sea and sky are of one tone
Where the sea drapes a lively skirt
Around the shape of islands
Where clouds stay one moment
Then give way to the sun

It rains one second
The next, clouds wipe away the darkness
Life flows slowly, slowly
On the islands

There is an island in the south
Waiting
No one but me can fill that space
The land that I discovered
A sun that burns my skin away
And heals the sores of winter
A wind that waves the softest hand

To calm the wildest palm trees

You think I'm dreaming?
You think I'm making up?
The endless green of islands?
You think I'm telling stories?
Some day I'll let you go
To see it for yourself
I'm not a dream, believe me
There is a tone of blue
That I cannot explain
You'd have to see it for yourself
Life glides slowly, slowly
On the islands

There is an island in the south
Where hours run longer than here
An island where no one has seen winter
Where sea and sky are of one tone

It's spring again, isn't it?
I'm going south.
I can't wait. My bus leaves tonight.
I can't miss it.

LEONOR
That could make a good story for a magazine.

VIRGINIA
What?

MADELINE
Wouldn't it make more sense to go south in winter, when it's cold here?

LEONOR
Madeline is interviewing me.

VIRGINIA
I'm sick and tired of welfare agents.
(*To MADELINE*) Did you come to inspect her home, to see if she qualifies?

LEONOR
She's not from Welfare.

VIRGINIA
I know. You're from the Health Department.

LEONOR *and MADELINE*
Wrong.

VIRGINIA
From the church. You do charity on your spare time.

LEONOR
It's an interview for a magazine.
(*To MADELINE*) Is that thing on? Turn it off. Erase that last part. You don't want to
keep al this nonsense.

MADELINE
It's all right. I have enough tape. Go ahead, be yourselves.

VIRGINIA
(*To LEONOR*) Can you lend me a couple of... ?

LEONOR
Is that why you came here?

VIRGINIA
I came to see how you were. It's just that I didn't get my check today. You know how
crazy the post office is getting.

LEONOR
No.

VIRGINIA
It's just a loan.

LEONOR
I have something to eat.

VIRGINIA
Where is it?

LEONOR
Hold it. I have to finish this interview first. It won't take long. Will it, Madeline?

MADELINE
No.

VIRGINIA
Something to drink?

LEONOR
Just water.

VIRGINIA
Something stronger?

LEONOR
I don't drink.

VIRGINIA
(*To MADELINE*) You have a cigarette? One of those whole ones?

MADELINE
I'm sorry. I don't smoke. I quit last year.

LEONOR
Good for you. Smoking gives you cancer.

VIRGINIA
I'm not afraid of that.

LEONOR
Virginia, weren't you on your way south? You're gonna miss your bus.

VIRGINIA
My bus leaves later tonight. I have a little time to spend with you, keep you company.
I came to say good-bye.

LEONOR
You never did that before. You just disappear.

VIRGINIA
This time I came.

LEONOR
Madeline and I are busy working on this interview. Do you mind?

VIRGINIA
I don't mind. Go ahead. I'm not in your way.

END OF SCENE 3

ACT I, SCENE 4

MADELINE
How long have you lived on the street?

LEONOR
Let me see. I came here in June. There is a place downtown where I stayed at the beginning. There were too many people so we had to take turns sleeping on the street. Later on I started coming around here. There is a better kind of people in this area. This spot is well lighted.

VIRGINIA
Six months ago I closed that door for good. I'm going back to visit, but not to stay. I can't be tied down. I like to move, I like adventure. I learn something in every country I visit.

LEONOR
You said that already.

MADELINE
What did you do before?

LEONOR
Before what?

MADELINE
Before now.

LEONOR
I am an actress. I don't practice anymore. All I was getting were the funny parts. I wanted to move on, do serious stuff, play important women like Marie Antoinette, Cleopatra, Eleanor Roosevelt. I get bored playing the same part every night. Monday through Friday. Weekends. It's a good idea to separate weeks from weekends. But you know what? Fridays are no different from Wednesdays. It's all up here. You know how the Sunday light looks different from the other days of the week? It isn't. one day runs into the next. They go on and on, and suddenly, you're old, your legs give out, you can't run anymore. This city is full of clocks. They light up at night. (*Points to a tower.*) That's my favourite one. Looks like a castle. City clocks ticking one after the other. You hear them? Tick, tick, tick. If they stop, you'll die. They're little time bombs in your head. Aren't they, Madeline?

MADELINE
Yes. Do you have any family?

LEONOR
I have a daughter. I lost track of her. Lost my glasses. That's why I can't read. I am divorced. I have the papers and everything. I was married to a bishop in the church. I married young. I didn't know what I was doing. He wasn't a bad man. It's just that he didn't have enough spirit. You know what I'm saying? It didn't work out. Just as well.

MADELINE
(*To VIRGINIA, who is writing on a pad.*) What are you writing?

VIRGINIA
I can't talk now. My dreams are coming back. I have to write them before I forget again.

LEONOR
Don't bother with her. She's not supposed to be here.
(*To VIRGINIA*) Your train is leaving soon.

VIRGINIA
My bus. I have a reservation. They have to wait for me. I have to finish this first. I keep a diary of my dreams. If I don't write them right away, I forget them. They're like silver fish that jump out for a second and sink back in the lake. I have to catch them before they go back.

LEONOR
Anyway, as I was saying, I used to work for the Treasury Department. I haven't turned in anyone lately. They give you a hundred and twenty dollars if you turn in

a bad person. I was after counterfeiters and people passing bad checks. I quit that.

MADELINE
Why?

LEONOR
I had to move around too much. Now I'm taking it easy. I'm my own boss now.

VIRGINIA
I had an operation in November. I didn't see the inside of a hospital for more than ten years. I just had another one. That should last me ten more.
I met a miner from Santa Barbara. He gave me a canary. I didn't have a cage for it. Now I travel light. Mining is a tough job. He used to tell me stories.

MADELINE
Where is he now?

LEONOR
I'm a Republican. Republicans have big bank accounts and government money. Republicans are good administrators, good planners. They always deal with a balanced budget. Democrats are good workers. I am a Republican.

MADELINE
Do you vote?

LEONOR
Of course not. I can't. I'm not registered.

VIRGINIA
(*Has put the pen and paper in a bag; she is now carefully examining pieces of materials, imagining them as pieces of jewelry.*) These are very pretty, but they don't match. Maybe if I dye them. I sell lots of these at the *Village Outdoor Exhibit.* They look for my stuff there. I have my own style. I'm not sure if I can go this summer. We'll see how things turn out. If I don't show up they're gonna keep the house. I'm not answering the letter. I have to see them in person. These (*pieces of plastic*) are too small. I can combine them with these. They make a good combination. Too much of the same don't look good.
(*Calls MADELINE away from LEONOR.*) Why do you bother with her? She's dirty.

MADELINE
Do you spend a lot of time on your feet?

LEONOR
I would say about eighty per cent.

VIRGINIA
I walk a lot, from the moment I wake up. My ass goes to sleep if I sit too much. I stay around main streets.

LEONOR
You meet lots of creeps in this city. It wasn't like this before. It's all those foreigners, them illegal aliens that are invading us. You know how you can tell them? They have funny accents. I can spot them (*snaps her fingers*) like that. They're not from here. They act different. One day I was sitting by the river, and I saw all these boat people, yellow and dark, making it upstream. Hundreds, thousands, millions of them. That's how they get in. The president doesn't even know they're here.

VIRGINIA
Sleeping is my favourite sport. I always dream. But I gotta be careful 'cause I get nightmares. I'm not afraid of nightmares; I live through them. I calm down when I start to understand what they're all about. I face my nightmares.

LEONOR
Isn't it nice to wake up and find out that it isn't really happening, that it was just a bad dream? It's a great feeling.

VIRGINIA
Last night: I'm walking up to here in water. I look back and I only see a wall. Someone is with me. I don't know who 'cause I'm looking somewhere else. I know it's a friend.

MADELINE
Man or woman?

VIRGINIA
(*Puts her beads away in silence.*) If I find a nice place to sleep I can dream about beautiful things. I've seen God.

MADELINE
How was God?

VIRGINIA
Kind of fuzzy. I'm walking down a dark, narrow, straight, long alley. Something is

pushing me gently. I know I shouldn't resist. I let myself go. Go. GO. My legs aren't even moving. I see a door at the end. I barely touch it. It opens. It's being pulled from the other side. It's the light. The incredible shine. No body or eyes, but I feel Him. I feel rested and secure. Endless happiness. Everything is clear now. I understand everything at once. I can remember everything that happened to me even before I was born. I know everything there is to know. (*Pauses*) A truck sprayed me and woke me up.

LEONOR
The Almighty has funny ways of bringing you back.

MADELINE
That's too bad. It was a beautiful dream. Are you religious?

LEONOR
I go to church in winter. They give out soup and sandwiches. I hate pea soup. I like minestrone with crackers. Hey give out blankets sometimes. I read the Bible. It's full of beautiful stories. I don't like the ending, though. I myself prefer happy endings. My mother read that book for dear life. She sat there and waited. She was ready. "It can come any moment," she said. "You have to be ready. The true life will begin any moment."

MADELINE
Where is she now?

Silence.

END OF SCENE 4

ACT I, SCENE 5

ANGELA *enters holding up her mat, on fire*
God will get your asses. (*Rushes in putting out her burning mat.*) I know who you are. (*At the top of her lungs.*) I'm gonna get you, wherever you hide. (*Inspects the mat.*) I'm gonna burn your houses down, you bastards. Those sons of bitches will pay for this.

LEONOR
What the hell is the matter with you now?

MADELINE
She looks upset.

ANGELA
(*To MADELINE*) You still here? I'm not answering any questions.

VIRGINIA
They burned her stuff.
(*To ANGELA*) You went in that park?

ANGELA
Don't ask me nothing.

LEONOR
They're always in that park. Night and day. They beat you, they rob you, they burn your things. I don't go in there anymore.

ANGELA
What's going on here?

MADELINE
Nothing. We're just chatting.

LEONOR
You're messing things up, you know?

ANGELA
Do you believe this? They burned everything. Where's my key? (*Searches for it frantically, finds it in her secret pocket.*) Here it is. (*Puts it back.*) They sprinkled fluid all over my car and put a match to it. Nobody paid no mind. It was a fucking joke to everybody. I could have killed all of them. If I get my hands on one of them, just one, I'd kill him.

LEONOR
Enough already. You're always killing somebody.

MADELINE
Why would anyone do such a thing?

VIRGINIA
For kicks, that's all. Those sons of bitches do it when they find nothing they want.

ANGELA *trying to repair the mat*
Look at it.

LEONOR
Take it easy. It's all over now. The whole thing is in the past now.

ANGELA
I don't want to remember anything. I want to forget what happened. She died, you know, just like that, right in front of my eyes.

MADELINE
Who died?

ANGELA
It's ruined.

LEONOR
It isn't. It's just a little corner. The rest is perfect. Besides, you can get a new one soon. Forget about it. It's easy. It will only take a second. (*Unloads a shopping cart from her carrier.*) This is for you. You can start all over right now. Put your things in there.

ANGELA
What things?

LEONOR *brings her the toaster*
You can start with this.

VIRGINIA *hands ANGELA a baby blue man's sweater.*
Take it. It's a little dirty but it's warm. It doesn't fit me anyway.

MADELINE
Hey, that color looks good on you.

ANGELA
Is that machine still on?

MADELINE
It's awful what they did to you.

ANGELA
What the hell do you care?

MADELINE
I understand what you feel.

ANGELA
The hell you do.

MADELINE
You're not alone. Many people that pass you in the street wonder who you are and why you're here.

ANGELA
I'm dying to kill you.

MADELINE
You have enough reason to be angry.

ANGELA
Why don't you tell them who you really are?

MADELINE
I had nothing to do with what happened.

ANGELA
Come on. Tell them. Who are you? Answer me, damn it.

MADELINE
I'm just trying to be friends.

ANGELA
I don't need friends. I'm better by myself.

VIRGINIA
(*To MADELINE*) Why would you want to be her friend?

LEONOR
So she can get information together. She's gonna sell an article on it.

VIRGINIA
You're gonna write all this?

MADELINE
The article is just part of it. I also want to get to know you, and how you live. I'm curious.

LEONOR
Curiosity killed the cat, they say.

MADELINE
I admire you, in a way.

ANGELA
Bullshit.

MADELINE
You are strong. You don't believe me, but I respect you. We have many things in common.

VIRGINIA
Like what?

MADELINE
We're all out here, dealing with this city. Things are constantly happening to us. I have been very scared of going out, but I know I have to, sometime. You have the spirit to live. I wish I could learn to make it. Like you.

LEONOR
Make it, make it. Make what? You sound like a creature from another planet.

VIRGINIA
You want to make it writing about us. You want to make some money on our stories. And what's in this for us, dear Madeline?

ANGELA
If you don't say right now who you are, I'm gonna tell them.

MADELINE
I come to learn from you. You're a free spirit. You have no program, no schedule, no obligations.

VIRGINIA
No food.

LEONOR
No money.

MADELINE
But you had the guts to choose your own life. You don't care what people think about you. So many people are hung up on that. Take me, for example. I became a writer five years ago. No, it's more like seven years. Before that, I was in a research program with the government. My life was totally different. I had a nine to five job. I was making tons of money. Then I decided to become a free lance writer and photographer. One day I stopped and said, "I'm going to do it." And I did it. I had to find my own way, do what I really enjoy doing. There are trade offs for all of us. We'd rather be out there than prisoners in a nine to five job that we hate and don't understand. We establish our own rules.

VIRGINIA
Rules are everywhere. You just better figure them out if you wanna stay around for a while.

LEONOR
Rules, chance, take your pick. It's all the same to me.
(*To MADELINE*) You live out here?

MADELINE
Yes. No. Uptown. Just a studio.

ANGELA
I'm not going to be part of this. I won't talk if that thing is on.

MADELINE
Sure. Let's turn it off. (*Turns it off.*)

ANGELA
Is it off now?

MADELINE
Yes, it's off.

ANGELA
You sure?

VIRGINIA
What's the big deal?

MADELINE
That's O.K. I understand. It's off, Angela.

ANGELA
What I say is not for the record. Leave me out, you understand? Forget I'm here. Just leave me alone. I'm not saying anything.

LEONOR
That's enough. Shut your mouth. Time for a break.

ANGELA goes to take a leak by the black plastic bags.

VIRGINIA
I'm starving. I want to eat something. I can't get on my bus with an empty stomach. It's a long trip.

LEONOR
Jesus, Virginia. You always want to be a step ahead of everybody. Take it easy. I have a surprise.

VIRGINIA
For me?

LEONOR
For everybody.

ANGELA
I hate surprises.

LEONOR
This is a good one.

ANGELA
So? Even if they're good... They catch you off guard.

LEONOR
Well, this one won't 'cause you know it's coming.

VIRGINIA
All right, get on with it. Surprises don't surprise me. I'm always ready for them.

END OF SCENE 5

END OF ACT I

ACT II, SCENE 6

LEONOR
(*Takes out the bag of chicken.*) Surprise! (*Starts setting a picnic on Angela's mat.*) Still hot.

ANGELA
Soggy. Where did you find it?

VIRGINIA
She stole it.

LEONOR
I don't steal.

VIRGINIA
Can't you take a joke?

LEONOR
I bought it this afternoon. My day wasn't bad.

ANGELA
Bullshit. They don't let you in there.

LEONOR
I sent someone.

ANGELA
I don't like this part. Do you have a leg?

LEONOR exchanges Angela's piece.

LEONOR
Madeline, help yourself.

MADELINE
Oh, no, thank you. I'm not hungry.

LEONOR
A piece of chicken fits anywhere. Go ahead. Don't be shy.

MADELINE
Really. I don't...

LEONOR
I bought it with my own money.

MADELINE
I don't mean that. It's just that I don't eat chicken. I'm a vegetarian.

LEONOR
That means she only eats vegetables.

VIRGINIA
No wonder she's so pale. It won't go to waste, believe me. There's plenty of room here
(*her stomach*). Any bread?

LEONOR throws her a roll.

VIRGINIA
(*To LEONOR*) Ketchup?

LEONOR
No ketchup today.

VIRGINIA
Pass the salt.

LEONOR
Madeline, french fries are vegetables. Have some.

MADELINE
Really, I'm not hungry. I ate just before coming here.

LEONOR
Suit yourself.
VIRGINIA
You can eat chicken with your fingers, you know?

LEONOR
Take it easy, Virginia. Don't eat so fast. It's bad for your digestion.

VIRGINIA
Don't worry about my digestion.

ANGELA

I've been here about five years. I had to leave that place. They put wires in your head. They stick needles in your veins. They give you cold showers and take your stuff away. They burn your things. I left that place a long time ago. I ain't going back, that's for sure.

LEONOR

We're not talking about that anymore. We're on our break now. What's the matter with you?

MADELINE

What was your life like before?

ANGELA

Before? I had bundles of money. My husband worked on Wall Street. He was good with money. I played the horses all the time. I went to the tracks every day.

VIRGINIA

Come on, tell the real story.

ANGELA

All right. I worked in a factory all my life. I made ladies blouses. Pants. Handbags.

VIRGINIA

She's lying.

ANGELA

All right. I came to this country when I was ten years old. My mother died the year after. No, a couple of years later. She couldn't make it here. She liked this city, but she couldn't handle it. They put me away. I couldn't speak the language. I didn't understand nothing. I got in trouble all the time. I kept telling them. I don't know where my father went, the bastard. I lost my cart. Some sons of bitches burned my things. Five years ago. Then I was a janitor for ten years. In an office. I don't want anyone near me. I can manage by myself. I don't want anybody touching me, like that Joe, the drummer, always trying to get on top of me. He's disgusting. I had a cat.

MADELINE

What was his name?

ANGELA'S SONG

I had the prettiest little cat
He was the smartest little kitten
His tail was black, his nose was white
His spotted body, lean and soft
He was my favorite company

His purr woke me in the morning
And helped me fall asleep at night
In winter, he would share my bed
He stayed under it in the summer

He ate with pleasure what I served
We always ate together
Raw eggs, and steak, and kidney
And for dessert
A plate of butter ice cream

He was the cleanest animal
I liked his independent style
He always found his way back to me
He knew I was the one who fed him

Then came a time we had to part
I could not keep him anymore
He didn't like the food I ate
He came to me on his own terms
He ate his food and walked away
He clawed my furniture and clothes
He shed his hair all over the place

I had this nasty animal
That bit my hand and ate my food
But now he's gone forever
I had a clever little pet
But one fine day he disappeared
I'm sure someone killed him
He died. I poisoned him.
The little bastard

LEONOR
(*To MADELINE*) So, you work for a magazine.

MADELINE
Not exactly. I'm just collecting information.

LEONOR
That's all? Is this your first job as a writer?

MADELINE
No. I've done other things in school.

LEONOR
Are you famous or something?

MADELINE
That's not easy in this city. You have to be in tune with the people; find out exactly what they want to know, otherwise they won't buy it.

LEONOR
I don't blame them.

ANGELA
You said that thing was off. You didn't turn it off like you said.

MADELINE
No, it's off. You see?

LEONOR
Do they pay you a salary?

MADELINE
Not exactly. You see, it's my business to write the article. When it's ready, I'll send it to different places.

LEONOR
That's what they call "investing," isn't it? You invest in your article now; it will pay you back later, right?

VIRGINIA
Any french fries?

LEONOR hands them to her with a dirty look.

VIRGINIA
They're cold.

MADELINE
I guess you can put it that way: an investment in myself. But aside from that, this is something I'm really interested in doing. Believe me, this is very important to me, even if I don't sell it.

LEONOR
No, no. Don't say that. Think positive.

MADELINE
I feel I've known you for a long time. I feel I've been here all my life.

LEONOR
You're starting to feel at ease, eh? You're learning.

VIRGINIA
Did you really learn something from what you saw and heard here?

MADELINE
I understand better.

VIRGINIA
Madeline, darling, would you be so kind as to lend me a couple of dollars? I don't usually do this, but this is an emergency. I'm leaving tonight and I'm short of cash. My check didn't come this week.

MADELINE
A couple of... Well, I guess... Sure, Virginia. (*Gives her a dollar.*) I don't have much.

VIRGINIA
Look at it as an investment. (*Licks her fingers.*) Leonor, this really hit the spot. It was a nice surprise. I could eat the bones.

ANGELA
You might as well.

VIRGINIA chews on the bones.

ANGELA *to MADELINE*
They burned all my money. I don't know how I'm gonna send money home this month.
I have to start all over again. I have to go uptown to get my money. See this key? It's for
a place where I keep my really important stuff. But I can't walk all the way there. Could
you help me out? It's a loan. I'll give it back to you as soon as I come back.

MADELINE
Angela, I would like to help, but I don't have money.

ANGELA
Forget it.

MADELINE *gives her money*
Take this, please. It's all I have.

LEONOR
You're a generous person. The money you give with one hand will come back to you
in the other. That's what my mother used to say. Charity is a great virtue.

MADELINE
I don't have money.

LEONOR
You could have saved some today by eating here. There is plenty of good food.

ANGELA
There was. This woman ate it all up. Look at her. You're a mess.

VIRGINIA
That's a lie. There's still a wing left. Anyone eating it?

MADELINE
No, thank you. You go ahead.

LEONOR
Hold it. (*Wraps it up.*) I'll save it for later. (*Puts it away.*)

VIRGINIA gets back to the bones.

LEONOR
It's too bad that place is closed. Otherwise, I'd send for coffee. Madeline, could you do me a favor?

VIRGINIA chokes on a bone and starts having convulsions. She cannot breath.

LEONOR *to ANGELA*
Slap her on the back.

MADELINE
She's choking.

LEONOR
It serves her right.

MADELINE
She can die.

LEONOR
She won't. She's been through many accidents. She always makes it.

ANGELA
She can't breathe.

MADELINE
We better call an ambulance. Is there a phone around here?

LEONOR
Around the corner.

MADELINE rushes out. LEONOR follows her a few steps.

LEONOR
In the candy store. Bring me a pack of cigarettes. *Virginia Slims*, no menthol. Those menthols give me a sore throat.

ANGELA hides MADELINE's tape recorder in her cart.

LEONOR
How is she doing?

ANGELA
She don't look good. She's turning colors.

LEONOR *shakes VIRGINIA*
Come on, woman. Breathe, breathe. (*Slaps her back.*) That's it. Get that chest moving. Come on. Go, go, go.

ANGELA
Stop it, Virginia. Don't die.

LEONOR
Your bus, Virginia, remember you gotta catch that bus. The south is waiting for you.

MADELINE returns.

MADELINE
The phone is out of order.

LEONOR
I didn't think you were coming back. Where are my cigarettes?

MADELINE
I forgot. Is she all right?

LEONOR
Leave her alone. She'll start breathing in a moment. She has to make it on her own.

MADELINE
We can't let her die like that. We have to do something. If you grab her around the chest, and close your fists together around her, and then push hard, it will come out. I saw it on TV.

ANGELA
You do it.

MADELINE does what she explained. It doesn't work.

MADELINE
What are we going to do?

LEONOR
Just wait. Everything will be all right.

MADELINE
She's going to die if we don't do something soon. My mother's cousin choked on a bone and they had to cut his throat open. He died anyway. It was too late.

LEONOR
Then get her out of here.

MADELINE
There must be a hospital around here somewhere.

LEONOR
Well, who's taking her?

MADELINE
I don't think I can. I'm sorry. I can't handle it.

LEONOR
Angela?

ANGELA
Not me. They won't let me in.

LEONOR
They will when they see she's dying.

ANGELA
I can't go there.

LEONOR
It's not you who's going in. You're helping a friend.

ANGELA
I don't know her that well.

LEONOR
You can handle it. You're a brave woman, come on, hurry. You're the only one who can do it.

ANGELA
I ain't leaving my things here.

LEONOR
Don't worry. I'll take good care of them. I'll be around for a while.

ANGELA carries VIRGINIA reluctantly. VIRGINIA is still coughing and kicking.

END OF SCENE 6

ACT II, SCENE 7

LEONOR
I'm dying for a cup of coffee.

MADELINE
I should have gone with them. She needed help. But I couldn't deal with it. I panic in situations like that. I don't have the strength. I'm useless in emergencies.

LEONOR
Nonsense. Angela can take care of the situation. Look, we did all we could. We slapped her on the back, we squeezed her chest. The rest is up to God and the experts. If her time has come, there's nothing we can do. If it hasn't, she'll be catching her bus soon.

MADELINE
She might die.

LEONOR
Stop the death talk. She won't. She hasn't died of worse things. I'm sure you can put all that in your story. It will spice it up. I can answer more questions now that there is some peace and quiet. There are other things I wanted to talk about before we were interrupted. For example...

MADELINE
Where's my tape recorder? (*She looks for it.*) It's not here. Not this, too.

LEONOR
I didn't touch it.

MADELINE
Then where is it?

LEONOR
Isn't that something? It was right here a while ago. This city is full of crooks. They hit and run.

MADELINE
That's all I need.

LEONOR
You're a professional. You must have a good memory. You heard everything that was said here, right? You were going to change things around anyway, so what's the difference? Just make it up. That's what writers do.

MADELINE
I'm not a professional. I'm not a writer. I'm a fake.

LEONOR
So, big deal.

MADELINE *takes out a pint of liquor and gulps a drink.*
They changed the lock to my apartment. They put my things out on the street. They said I was three months behind with my rent. That's not true. I lost my receipts, so I couldn't prove anything. They sent me letters to appear in court, but I was sick. I couldn't show up. This morning I took my tape recorder with me. I was going to make some money singing out there, but it didn't work out. I only had ten dollars that a man gave me.

LEONOR
Ten dollars.

MADELINE
I spent most of it. (*Drinks.*) I didn't know where to go. I've been walking around. Now my tape recorder is gone, too. Everything gone in one day. (*Drinks.*) You know, I was very fond of that machine. I've had it for many years. It gave me many hours of pleasure. I feel great when I sing. You seem to have it all together. I want to learn from you.

LEONOR
First lesson: forget everything you heard here. It will be of no use to you. Be on the move all the time.

MADELINE
I haven't talked to anyone in a long time. Really talk, you know what I'm saying? I got fed up with my bosses at the shipping company. Each had a different set of rules. One told me to do things one way; the other came to tell me I was doing it wrong. They fired me. I cracked up right in the office in front of everybody. Lucky they let me get unemployment. That carried me for a while. Temporaries were the solution for another while. I did so many things at so many different places that looked the same. I kept running into the same boss over and over. One day I walked out for good. I sent home some desperate letters which got me some money, but I couldn't go back. I had to face that I was a big girl now, on my own. Once I leave something I don't look back. Anywhere, but back. I held on to that apartment as long as I could. I made the rules in there. I looked at the world through my television. When I didn't like what was happening in the world, I changed channels. I could get away with a click. Click: I'm in the African jungle. Click: I'm in the bottom of the sea with Jacques Cousteau. Click: I'm traveling in space. Click: I'm a sexy woman singing, dancing, and laughing.

LEONOR
Click: you are here now.

MADELINE
It's strange to just float around.

LEONOR
Soon it will be spring. It's a matter of days. So, you feel like a turtle belly side up. You just have to keep trying to turn around and keep going. You have the guts.

MADELINE
That's the thing: I don't. I tried everything. I took courses in journalism, speed-reading, modelling. I thought I was prepared. I thought I had the talent. God knows I tried.

LEONOR
He don't know. He's busy somewhere else.

MADELINE
I studied music. I have a good singing voice. I'm a mezzo.

LEONOR
You sing? What kind of music?

MADELINE
Folk, classical, popular. I'm well trained, but I'm missing something. I can't stand be-

ing judged. I can't compete. I fail all auditions.

LEONOR
Are you hungry?

MADELINE
I had a cup of coffee this morning.

LEONOR gives her the chicken wing.

MADELINE
I had recorded two hours of music to sing by. I tried singing out here this morning for the first time. I was petrified. I stood straight, closed my eyes, waited for the applause to quiet down. The house was still. I pushed the play button and sang.

LEONOR
Did you make any money?

MADELINE
The police gave me a ticket for loitering.

LEONOR
Throw it away. You don't have to pay it.

MADELINE *takes out her music tape*
I have the tape here, but what good is it? The machine is gone. (*Throws tape away.*)

LEONOR
Don't do that. Save it. You never know. You can sing without music until you make enough money to get a new one. Or you might find one around. (*Puts cassette back in MADELINE's hand.*) Those bags are full of surprises. People leave behind many treasures. You have to learn where to look. The Garment District is not bad. That's where I got this home (*the carrier*). You can pick up good stuff around there. The Chelsea area doesn't have good restaurants, although it's picked up a little in the last couple of years. The restaurants around the east thirties are so-so. This chicken place right there has its good and bad days. Things are better uptown: Fifth Avenue, Madison, Park... but don't go beyond 96th Street. That's something else up there. This city is many cities. You turn the corner and find yourself among strangers. You know, I've been here so long that I forgot where I came from. I'm from here.

LEONOR'S SONG

This is my home, my family. Here's everything I want.

Every little thing in here is in my mind, too.
I know where everything is,
What I have left and what I left behind.

This is my home, my family. Here's everything I own.

This evening dress used to belong
To a sad lady of the East Side.
This music box used
To put the kids asleep;
Now it only plays the music of my mind.
This pan belonged to a famous Chinese-Cuban cook
Who went back to China.
This button fell off the coat
Of the Iranian Ambassador's chauffer.
His car was towed away.
Postcards for lovers who never got them.
I wonder where they went.
This bread is for the birds
That wait for me in every park.
Cigarettes for my friends
When they need to relax.
(I'm out of them this time.)
These newspapers are warm.
This broom was picked up by a friend who went away.
You like the color?
These curtains used to hang in a Broadway theater.
(Puts her ear to the curtain.)
Hear the applause?
Pretty, soft, looked at many times.
They used to rise and fall
In front of marvellous worlds.
This chair came from a school.
It's carved with many names.

This is my home, my family. I know everything is here.

Things flow into my open hands.
I let them in and let them out.

MADELINE
I feel a personal kind of relationship to you.

LEONOR
Don't. We won't be here tomorrow. Take what you can now.

MADELINE
It looks like it's going to rain.
LEONOR
I'm afraid so.

MADELINE
What will you do?

LEONOR
I don't know.

MADELINE
You don't care about the future.

LEONOR
I don't care about what happened already or what hasn't happened yet. If it already happened, there's nothing I can do about it, so why worry? You can't believe everything the weather bureau tells you. If you worry about rain and it don't rain, you worry for nothing. I have plastic covers for everything. I move around: my home is here, my bathroom is over there, in the subway. I never know where I'm gonna have my next coffee. It always comes. Things happen anyway.

END OF SCENE 7

ACT II, SCENE 8

ANGELA rushes in and goes directly to her cart. VIRGINIA follows shortly.

ANGELA
She didn't want to go.

VIRGINIA
I'm all right. It was nothing. They would have cut my throat open in there. People go in that hospital and come out feet first.

LEONOR
How did it happen?

VIRGINIA
It came out by itself.

ANGELA
Right in front of the hospital. I was pushing her in.

VIRGINIA
You have any water?

LEONOR hands her the bottle. VIRGINIA drinks avidly.

LEONOR
I knew it. You see? She's breathing and everything.

MADELINE
Thank goodness.

ANGELA
She's still here.

LEONOR
She couldn't leave without her machine. It disappeared.

ANGELA
She ain't gonna write about me, then.

LEONOR
She's no writer. She's a singer.

VIRGINIA
I knew it. I have a thing for faces. You didn't look like a writer to me. (*Takes a closer look.*) Yes, you could be a singer.

LEONOR
You fooled me. You sounded just like that woman who interviewed me last year. No, more than a year ago. Much more. When nobody knew who I was, she took a picture. People recognize me from that picture. People stop me in the street to ask me, "Are you so and so?" To me, you looked just like that writer. Listen, Madeline, maybe you should go in a different direction. You say you can sing. Come on, sing something.

MADELINE
Now? I can't. I'm not prepared.

LEONOR
Sure you are.

MADELINE
What shall I sing?

LEONOR
Anything. She needs her background music. Angela, can we borrow your machine?

ANGELA
What machine?

LEONOR
You know, that little machine that grabs your words. That little machine that remembers everything you say.

ANGELA
I don't have anything like that.

VIRGINIA
So that's how she did it. She told me she took her words back from Madeline.

MADELINE
Angela, please, that machine is all I have.

ANGELA *gets her knife out and attacks MADELINE*
Get away from me. If you come closer I'll kill you. She's the devil.

LEONOR
Nobody's gonna take your words. You can have them back. That's what you want, isn't it? I'll show you how to get them back. Where's the machine? Is it there?

ANGELA
Don't touch my property.

LEONOR
I'm not touching anything. You're gonna give me the machine and I'm gonna show you where the words are.

MADELINE
Can I explain something? All she has to do is...

LEONOR
Shut up, you fool. Don't say a word. She'll get over it. She gets nervous sometimes. She has a short fuse, that's all. Angela, is it there with that beautiful toaster I gave you?

ANGELA
I found it myself.

LEONOR
That's right, you found that toaster yourself. It's beautiful. I wish I had one like that.

ANGELA takes out the machine. She looks at it for a moment, then hands it over to LEONOR. LEONOR opens it and pulls out the cassette. She pulls out the tape and holds it up to ANGELA's eyes.

LEONOR
Your words are stuck to this tape. (*ANGELA looks for them.*) You can't see them, but they're there, stuck to it somehow.

MADELINE
You can erase it. All you have to do is...

LEONOR
Shut your mouth. Don't say nothing. She's not going to believe you. Here, you can

have your words back. They're all yours. (*ANGELA destroys the tape.*) Now, you see? The machine is empty. No words in there. Now we'll give it back to Madeline so she can put her music in there. And she's gonna sing for us. Aren't you, Madeline?

MADELINE
Now?

LEONOR
Right now.

ANGELA
What is she going to sing?

LEONOR
A very happy song. Aren't you, Madeline?

MADELINE
I can't sing now.

LEONOR
Of course you can. Sing a happy one, O.K.?

MADELINE puts the cassette in the machine.

LEONOR
Hit it, Madeline.

MADELINE'S SONG

This house is shaking.
I hear it humming.

This house is making a noise
That no one hears.

We won the fight against February.
The birds are bringing back spring.

This house is humming.
I saw a tree in the park

Take out its flowers in public light.

This house is shaking.
I hear it humming.
The air is singing inside.

This house is making a noise
That no one hears
But me.

We made it, we made it.
Spring is here.

LEONOR and VIRGINIA applaud.

MADELINE
Thank you. I wrote that song myself.

ANGELA
Was that a happy song?

LEONOR
You have many talents.

VIRGINIA
That could be a good act. But you have to sing out with confidence. Open your eyes and stare out. Pick out someone in the audience and sing to that person alone. Then change to another person. You have to reach the individual.

LEONOR
She should do something with her hands. Move her head a little, you know what I mean? She's too stiff. She needs a little movement to pick it up. You have a good voice.

VIRGINIA
Not bad at all. Listen, I have to go. I just came back to let you know I'm fine. My bus is waiting. I hate to make people wait. I want nothing else to happen. I knew something was going to happen to me when that truck splashed me. It was a sign. I should have left the city right away. Instead I came here to say good-bye. I'm getting out right now. But first I want to freshen up a bit. Some water?

LEONOR gives her the bottle. She washes her face and hands. MADELINE takes a drink and passes the bottle to VIRGINIA.

VIRGINIA *drinks*
Just what I needed.

LEONOR *takes out a magazine*
Let me show you something.

MADELINE *reads*
"Street People."

LEONOR
That's it. You read it out loud. I lost my glasses.

VIRGINIA lights the cigarette she had put away "for the road" and shares it with LEONOR.

MADELINE
"Identifying an individual as a street dweller is a subjective and inexact task. We depended upon physical appearance, behavior, and presence in the same general area over a period of days or weeks. People who carry excessive or inappropriate belongings for an extended period of time, who wore shabby or poorly fitting clothes, or who dressed unseasonably (many are probably anaemic, and may wear several topcoats even during summer) were considered as candidates for study. Lea (a pseudonym) told us that she occasionally slept with several other women. This atypical group was formed for warmth and protection."

VIRGINIA and MADELINE have another round of drinks. ANGELA polishes the toaster. LEONOR puts on her warm socks.

MADELINE *continues*
"They're very much like us. Curiosity was my main reason to conduct the interviews. Here's a subgroup of our society who has had the guts to do something many of us are unable to do. They're living a freer, more independent kind of life. In some way, because of our hang-ups, we tend to fantasize about them, thinking that these bag men and ladies are sitting on bundles of money. That's not true in most cases. I realized that these people have a pattern to their lives which is not that different from ours. We go to the bank in the morning to take out money on our way to work; they collect theirs at a corner of their choice."

There's a huge two-page spread of you, Leonor.

LEONOR *looks at the picture*
There I am. I told you. (*Pauses.*) Time to move on. (*Starts gathering her belongings.*)
I'm gonna get some nice hot coffee.

VIRGINIA *looks at Leonor's favorite clock up in the tower*
Time for me to go. My bus is about to leave. I can't stay with you any longer.

LEONOR
Have a nice trip.

VIRGINIA
You too.

LEONOR
Careful where you fall asleep.

VIRGINIA *exiting*
See you next winter.

LEONOR
Maybe.

ANGELA
This (*impeccably polished toaster*) is nice.

LEONOR
Yeah, so shiny.

*ANGELA carefully places her toaster in her cart and gets on her way. The squeaky wheel
makes movement difficult.*

LEONOR
Hey, what happened to your eclipse?

ANGELA
I'll catch it some other time.

LEONOR
She's calmed down. She has some temper. Madeline, I hate to bother you, but can I
borrow some change for a cup of coffee?

MADELINE
I gave Angela and Virginia all I had.
LEONOR
That's all right. Forget I asked.

MADELINE
Wait a minute. (*Takes out her last dollar.*) I was saving this. It's all I've left.

LEONOR snatches it from her hand.

LEONOR
This should be enough. Thank you. You're a generous person. Good luck in your new career. See you around. And remember, keep your eyes open when you sing.

LEONOR exits. MADELINE finds something to eat in the bags, sits by the bank entrance, and rehearses her song.

MADELINE *sings*
This house is shaking.
I hear it humming.

The air is singing inside.

This house is making a noise
That no one hears but me.

We made it, we made it.
Spring is here.

As lights dim, the sign that reads "A new concept in banking" becomes evident.

END OF PLAY